Stefan Forster Architekten

Wohnungsbau
Housing
1989–2019

PARK BOOKS

Vorwort • Foreword	20
Michael Mönninger: Die Würde des Wohnens • The Dignity of Housing	22

Städtischer Block
City Block

Lagepläne • Site plans	40
Schwarzwaldblock, Mannheim	45
Schwedler-Carré 01, Frankfurt am Main	57
Wohnanlage Voltastraße • Voltastraße residential development, Frankfurt am Main	73
Markgrafenkarree, Berlin	85

Haus in der Stadt
City Building

Lagepläne • Site plans	94
Gemeindezentrum • Community Centre, Frankfurt am Main	101
Westgarten 01, Frankfurt am Main	113
Oskar Residence, Frankfurt am Main	125
Campus Bockenheim, Frankfurt am Main	137
Schloßstraße, Frankfurt am Main	149
Sandweg, Frankfurt am Main	161
Wohnen auf Naxos • Living on Naxos, Frankfurt am Main	169
Adickesallee, Frankfurt am Main	177
Ostendstraße, Frankfurt am Main	185
Windeckstraße, Frankfurt am Main	193
R7, Mannheim	201
Unterrather Straße, Düsseldorf	209
Französische Allee, Hanau	217

Siedlung
Housing Estate

Lagepläne • Site plans	226
Wohnen im Park • Houses in the park, Frankfurt am Main	229
Mainzeile, Offenbach am Main	241
Riedberg 04, Frankfurt am Main	249

Transformation

Lagepläne • Site plans	258
Lyoner Straße 01, Frankfurt am Main	263
Philosophicum, Frankfurt am Main	275
Haus 01–06, Leinefelde	291
Haus 07, Leinefelde	307
Haus 08, Halle (Saale)	315

Hausgrundrisse
Floor plans 1:200

	324
Büro • Office	336
Projektübersicht • Project overview	337
Preise • Awards	340
Abbildungsnachweis • Illustration credits	341
Impressum • Publication details	342

Seit seiner Gründung 1989 widmet sich unser Büro dem Wohnungsbau. In all den Jahren begleitete uns immer wieder der Gedanke, ein Resümee unseres bisherigen Architekturschaffens zu ziehen. Die vorliegende Monografie nimmt sich dieser Aufgabe an: Sie dokumentiert 30 exemplarische Bauten aus 30 Jahren architektonischer Praxis des Büros *Stefan Forster Architekten* und versteht sich zugleich als Beitrag zur Debatte um Qualitäten im Wohnungsbau. Der schlichte wie universelle Titel »Wohnungsbau 1989–2019« ist durchaus programmatisch zu verstehen. So schlägt das Buch einen Bogen vom sozialen Wohnungsbau zum aufwändigen Eigentumswohnungsbau, von der Siedlung zum verdichteten Bauen im gemischten Stadtquartier und vom Stadthaus auf der Parzelle zum Großblock.

Aufmerksam reflektieren wir dabei die unterschiedlichen sozialen und politischen Bedingungen des Wohnens an prägenden Bauten: So stand die Transformation von Plattenbauten im Zuge des Stadtumbaus Ost in Leinefelde und Halle an der Saale noch ganz im Zeichen des zunehmenden Leerstands und der Abwanderung großer Teile der Bevölkerung. Auf der anderen Seite des Spektrums befinden sich hingegen die prosperierenden Großstädte und Ballungszentren, deren Wachstum mit weitreichenden Fragen an Architektur und Städtebau verbunden ist. Beispielhafte Strategien für die Bewältigung dieser neuen Wohnungskrise zeigen Projekte wie die verdichteten kommunalen Großblocks – etwa in Mannheim und Frankfurt am Main (Schwarzwaldblock, Wohnanlage Voltastraße) – oder die Umwandlung leerstehender Büro- und Verwaltungsgebäude in neuen Wohnraum (Lyoner Straße 01, Philosophicum).

Der Aufbau dieser Publikation folgt dem architektonischen Gedanken einer Bewegung vom Maßstab der Stadt über die Ausgestaltung des einzelnen Bauwerks bis hin zum Grundriss der Wohnung bzw. des Hauses. Der Auftakt umfasst eine Bildserie der Fotografin Lisa Farkas, die sich den Stadträumen um einige unserer Frankfurter Projekte widmet. In dem Essay »Die Würde des Wohnens« betrachtet der Kunsthistoriker Michael Mönninger anschließend die Wohnungsfrage als Spiegel sozialer und historischer Veränderungen und unternimmt aus dieser Perspektive den Versuch einer Positionsbestimmung des Büros *Stefan Forster Architekten*.

Den Kern dieser umfangreichen Monografie bildet eine ausführliche Projektdarstellung, die typologisch in vier Kapitel gegliedert ist. Darin wird die Darstellung der klassischen Bautypen des städtischen Blocks, des Stadthauses und der Siedlung in einem weiteren Kapitel um unterschiedliche Transformationsprojekte ergänzt. Neben der Architekturfotografie, für die Lisa Farkas und Jean-Luc Valentin verantwortlich zeichnen, haben wir eigens für dieses Buch eine umfangreiche Hintergrundrecherche unternommen. Den Beginn jedes Projekts markiert eine Klappseite, die als »Wundertüte« ergänzende und weiterführende Materialien enthält und eine Kontextualisierung der Projekte ermöglichen soll.

Dieses Buch ist auch als Plädoyer für eine qualitätsvolle Alltagsarchitektur im bewussten Gegensatz zu einer ikonografischen Look-at-me-Architektur zu verstehen. Die Qualität unserer Arbeit, die sich der langjährigen Definition und Weiterentwicklung von Standards im Wohnungsbau verdankt, wäre ohne ein engagiertes Team undenkbar. Mein Dank gilt deswegen den über 150 Mitarbeiterinnen und Mitarbeitern, die uns in dieser Zeit begleitet haben, meinem Partner Florian Kraft, seit 2013 Geschäftsführer von *Stefan Forster Architekten*, sowie all unseren Partnerinnen und Partnern. Nach einem Ausspruch von Erich Mendelsohn besteht die Existenz des Architekten in der lebenslangen Suche nach dem richtigen Bauherrn. Insofern ist dieses Buch auch eine Danksagung an all die Bauherren, die mit qualitätsvoller Architektur einen Beitrag zu einer gelungenen Stadtentwicklung leisten.

From the outset in 1989, our practice has focused on housing construction. In the years since then we have often considered the idea of producing a review of our architectural projects. The present monograph addresses this task. It documents 30 buildings that exemplify the work of *Stefan Forster Architekten* over 30 years of architectural practice, and is at the same time a contribution towards the debate about quality in housing construction. Under the simple and programmatic title of "Housing 1989–2019", it traces a wide arc from social housing to expensive freehold apartments, from housing estates to denser developments in mixed urban districts, and from individual buildings in the city to large perimeter blocks.

In this resumé we reflect on the different social and political context of housing, as illustrated by key building projects: In Leinefelde and Halle an der Saale, for example, the transformation of old, panel-built residential buildings (*Plattenbauten*) was prompted by a major regeneration programme for urban areas in the former GDR, in response to the exodus of large parts of the population and a rising number of empty apartments. On the other side of the spectrum there are the flourishing cities and conurbations whose continued expansion raises far-reaching questions as regards architecture and urban planning. Examples of successful strategies for managing this new housing crisis can be found in the projects that focus on increasing the density of development in large municipal housing projects, such as in Mannheim and Frankfurt (Schwarzwaldblock, Voltastraße residential development) – or the transformation of empty office and administration buildings into new residential accommodation (Lyoner Straße 01, Philosophicum).

In terms of structure, this publication follows the architectural idea of moving from the scale of the city to the design of the individual building, and then on to the plan for the apartment or building. The scene is set by a series of images by photographer Lisa Farkas who explored the urban spaces around a few of our projects in Frankfurt. Then, in an essay entitled "The Dignity of Housing", art historian Michael Mönninger examines the question of housing as a mirror of social and historical change and, from this perspective, ventures an appraisal of the guiding philosophy behind the work of *Stefan Forster Architekten*.

The main section of this comprehensive monograph is dedicated to a detailed presentation of each of the 30 projects, divided typologically into four chapters. As well as the classical categories of the city block, the individual building in the city and the housing estate, there is also a range of projects that come under the heading of transformation. Specially for this publication we commissioned architectural photographs from Lisa Farkas and Jean-Luc Valentin and conducted extensive background research. A fold-out page, with supplementary material, marks the start of each project description, giving the reader an opportunity to find out more about the respective context.

This book can also be seen as testimony to the value of quality in architecture for the everyday, in deliberate contrast to an iconographic "look at me" style of architecture. The quality of our work, which is based on a long process of definition and further development of standards in housing construction, could never have been achieved without a dedicated team. I am greatly indebted therefore to the over 150 employees who have worked with us in this time, to Florian Kraft, partner and managing director in the practice since 2013, and to all our external partners. In the words of Erich Mendelsohn, an architect can spend his entire working life searching for the right client. In this light therefore, this monograph is also an expression of gratitude to all those "right clients" who through their support for quality architecture have made a positive contribution to the urban environment.

Die Würde des Wohnens. Über die Häuser des Büros Stefan Forster Architekten

Michael Mönninger

»Des Menschen Wohnung ist sein halbes Leben.«
(J. W. v. Goethe)[1]

Wenn es ein Leitmotiv der modernen Architektur im 20. Jahrhundert gab, dann war es die Lösung der Wohnungsfrage. Jede Architektengeneration träumte von sozialpolitischen Großtaten und entwarf mit bemerkenswertem Pathos immer effizientere Haus- und Wohnungsgrundrisse. Heraus kamen dabei Gebäude mit exakt definierten Tätigkeitsflächen entlang spezialisierter Raumzuschnitte, die nicht nur das Bauen rationalisieren, sondern auch das Nutzerverhalten regulieren sollten.[2] Nach hundert Jahren dieser ergonomisch optimierten Erziehungsarchitektur ist das Resultat enttäuschend: Viele Siedlungen und Neustädte – vor allem aus der zweiten Hälfte des 20. Jahrhunderts – entwickeln sich zu hochsubventionierten Behältern des sozialen Notstands, die Einfamilienhausteppiche werden zu Rentnerkolonien und wer kann, wohnt im sogenannten Altbau.

Allerdings macht die Baualtersklasse aus der Zeit vor 1918 nur noch zwanzig Prozent des deutschen Wohnungsbestandes aus, sodass großer Bedarf an neuen Häusern besteht, die sowohl traditionelle Ansprüche an Dauerhaftigkeit und Nutzungsvielfalt erfüllen als auch der modernen Auffächerung der Lebensstile Rechnung tragen. Die übersichtliche Alltagsrealität des industriegeschichtlichen Fordismus mit regulärem Acht-Stunden-Tag ist ebenso vorbei wie das geschlossene Familienmodell, in dem ein erwerbstätiger Vater die Hausfrau und Mutter mit zwei Kindern ernährte. Sie bildeten die Grundstruktur, welche die soziale Stadt- und Wohnungspolitik im 20. Jahrhundert architektonisch prägte.

Heute sind es Singles und Alleinerziehende, Deutsche mit und ohne Migrationshintergrund, Doppelverdiener mit und ohne Kinder, die den Alltag der deutschen Gesellschaft bestimmen. Hinzu kommen Patchworkfamilien mit dem Nachwuchs verschiedener Partner sowie eine wachsende Gruppe multipler Dienstleister, die an den wechselnden Orten ihrer Arbeit ein Appartement suchen. Zudem wächst die Nachfrage nach Mehr-Generationen-Wohnformen, die der veränderten Demografie der deutschen Methusalem-Gesellschaft Rechnung tragen. Denn 2050 wird die Hälfte der Deutschen über 60 Jahre alt sein, sodass das Zusammengehen der Generationen wie in der vorindustriellen Epoche eine Lösung vieler alltagspraktischer Probleme bietet.

Für die Architektur bedeutet dieser Wandel, dass sie sich nicht mehr auf ein normiertes Modell des Wohnens beziehen kann, sondern mit einer Vielfalt individueller Verhaltensweisen sowie vernetzten und interaktiven Wohnwelten konfrontiert ist. Doch steht der neuen Pluralität und Biegsamkeit der Lebensformen eine groteske Starrheit des bisherigen Wohnungsangebotes gegenüber.

Wahrnehmung durch Gewöhnung

Der Frankfurter Architekt Stefan Forster würde dieser Kritik der heutigen Wohnversorgung sicherlich zustimmen, ohne jedoch angesichts der Auflösung sozialer Rollenmodelle auch die Verflüssigung der architektonischen Form zu fordern. Experimente im Wohnungsbau mit flexiblen Wänden auf wandelbaren Grundrissen in biomorph geformten Kapseln, die in freistehende Tragkonstruktionen eingehängt werden und für transitorische Zweckbestimmungen umrüstbar sein sollen, überlässt Forster lieber anderen. Er hält nichts von der Suche nach dem zielgruppengerechten und maßgeschneiderten Bauen, das sich transparent, beweglich und verschiebbar allen wechselnden Ansprüchen und Vitalfunktionen der Bewohner anpasst. Dagegen setzt er seine Auffassung von Anonymität, Alltäglichkeit, Neutralität, Serialität und Dauerhaftigkeit im Bauen. Für ihn ist ein Gebäude gelungen, wenn es seine Bewohner überdauert, für 90 Prozent der Bevölkerung brauchbar ist und ohne den Widmungsterror von speziellen Nutzungszuschreibungen auskommt.

Die Nüchternheit der Bauauffassung von Stefan Forster und seinen Architekten zeigt sich schon beim ersten Anblick der Häuser. Die Gebäude sollen bei den Betrachtern einen Déjà-vu-Effekt erzeugen, als hätten sie diese irgendwo schon einmal gesehen, ohne sagen zu können, ob sie vor fünf oder fünfzig Jahren gebaut worden sind. Auch wer die Referenzen nicht kennt, soll die Bauten als vertraut empfinden. Dieser fundamentale Wiedererkennungseffekt geht weit über die individuelle Entwurfshaltung eines Architekturbüros hinaus. Er beruht vielmehr auf der elementarästhetischen Sinnestätigkeit der Gewöhnung, welche die Grundlage des Wohnens ist.

Das meinte Walter Benjamin mit seiner Beobachtung, Architektur werde auf doppelte Art rezipiert: durch Wahrnehmung und Gebrauch, also optisch und taktil. Die optische Wahrnehmung, etwa beim Anblick berühmter Bauwerke, geschieht Benjamin zufolge auf dem Wege der Kontemplation, zu der es jedoch auf der taktilen Gebrauchsseite der Alltagsarchitektur keine Entsprechung gibt; hier erfolge die Rezeption vielmehr auf dem Wege der Gewohnheit. Dem gespannten Aufmerken der Kontemplation und Sammlung steht laut Benjamin also das beiläufige Bemerken durch Gewohnheit und Zerstreuung gegenüber, bei dem weniger der Augenschein als der Bewegungs- und Berührungssinn angesprochen werde.[3] An Benjamins Gedanken einer latenten Wirkungsweise von Architektur, die auf dem Wege der Habitualisierung angeeignet wird, knüpft die neuere Wahrnehmungs- und Architekturtheorie an. Sie behandelt die leibbezogene »Nebenbei-Wahrnehmung« von Gebautem als implizite, unbewusste Interaktion von Individuum und Umwelt, bei der die direkte Wahrnehmung stets durch indirekte Vorhersagen und Erinnerungen erweitert wird.[4]

Doch werden diese unterschwelligen Qualitäten von Gebäuden, die sich in Alltagsroutinen erschließen und – mit Langzeitfolgen für die Lebensqualität – meist Hintergrundphänomene bleiben, in der Theorie und Praxis des Bauens selten thematisiert. Wenn Architekten heute an Gedächtnis und Erinnerung appellieren, dann meinen sie weniger die Aneignung durch Gewohnheit und Gebrauch, sondern den Griff in den Fundus der Baugeschichte. Sie zitieren mit Vorliebe historische Formen und Bilder, die zwar kontemplative Aufmerksamkeit auf sich ziehen, aber weniger für den beiläufigen Dauergebrauch mit allen Sinnen geeignet sind. Solche Veduten können Emotionen mobilisieren, aber keine Energien.

Schrumpfkur des modernen Wohnens

Auch Stefan Forster und sein Büro verwenden Bezüge aus der Architekturgeschichte der Frühmoderne und der Zwischenkriegszeit vor hundert Jahren. Aber sie bleiben nicht bei der Reproduktion neusachlicher Kubaturen und expressionistischer Oberflächen stehen, sondern fragen zugleich, wie sich die Irrtümer und Fehlentwicklungen, die der heroischen Moderne im Wohnungsbau unterlaufen sind, heute korrigieren lassen. Denn die Vertreter des internationalen *Neuen Bauens* nach dem Ersten Weltkrieg setzten mit ihren Idealentwürfen für Stadterweiterungen und Siedlungen jene Schrumpfkur fort, die das menschliche Wohnen in der Neuzeit dadurch erfahren hat, dass alle traditionellen Routinen und sozialen Verschränkungen auseinandergerissen wurden. Erst verschwand die Arbeit aus dem Haushalt, dann wurden alle Personen ausgeschlossen, die nicht zur Kernfamilie gehörten – von Hilfskräften bis hin zu Großeltern. Anstelle von Allzweckräumen entstanden separate Wohnbereiche – für jede Funktion und Person. So entwickelten sich Wohnungen schließlich zu miniaturisierten Inseln privater, intimer Geborgenheit, die der Öffentlichkeit maximal entzogen waren.

Diese Introvertiertheit präsentierte sich außen in antistädtischen Siedlungen mit undifferenzierten Grünflächen und Freiräumen für ein gesäubertes Freizeitdasein. Die Trabantenstädte und Hochhausensembles nach dem Zweiten Weltkrieg brachten mit der totalen Vergesellschaftung des Planens, Bauens und Wohnens schließlich das genaue Gegenteil hervor: ein Höchstmaß an Privatheit. Denn der sozialen Unterforderung der Menschen in der gestapelten individuellen Kleinfamilienwohnung entsprach ihre Überforderung in der Summe der kollektiven Großwohnanlage. Maximale Isolation und zugleich totale Integration, so die damalige Wohnforschung, hinterließen bei den Bewohnern ein Gefühl der »Schutzlosigkeit und Distanzlosigkeit« sowohl gegenüber dem architektonischen als auch dem sozialen Umfeld.[5]

Dem überspezialisierten Superfunktionalismus des entmischten Wohnungs- und Siedlungsbaus kann die heutige Architektur keine Idealentwürfe entgegensetzen. Voll integrierte urbane Hauswirtschaften mit umfassender ökonomischer Teilhabe und sozialer Kooperation wird es auch deshalb nicht mehr geben, weil niemand auf die unbestreitbaren Emanzipationsgewinne verzichten möchte, welche die Befreiung aus den alten Haushierarchien und Wohnabhängigkeiten gebracht haben. Dennoch kann die Moderne durchaus zur historischen Selbstkritik fähig sein, um auch aus dem Reservoir der Geschichte tragfähige Wohn- und Stadtstrukturen zusammenzubauen.

Weil sich die vagabundierenden, verflüssigten Lebensverhältnisse heute vom Haus gelöst haben, wird nach den Worten des Berliner Stadtplaners und Architekturtheoretikers Dieter Hoffmann-Axthelm das wichtigste Kriterium künftiger Urbanität sein, »wie viele funktionale und soziale Stränge ein Gebäude aus der modernen Isolierung heraus wieder miteinander verknüpfen kann«.[6] Damit beschreibt er die Herausforderung, bislang ausgelagerte Funktionen – etwa Arbeit und Versorgung, Kinder- und Altenbetreuung – in das Wohnumfeld zurückzuholen. Nach einem Jahrhundert der Vergesellschaftung und Externalisierung nahezu aller Funktionen des Wohnens geht es nun um die Wiedergewinnung von Selbstverantwortung und sozialer Autonomie.

Rückbau und Ausbau

Solche Qualitäten sind im heutigen Wohnungsbau nur selten realisierbar. Dennoch sollte man froh sein, wenn Architektinnen und Architekten wissen, wie groß die Fallhöhe zwischen historisch-theoretischem Anspruchsniveau und realer Baupraxis ist. Für Stefan Forster war die Konfrontation mit dem 2002 aufgelegten Bund-Länder-Förderprogramm »Stadtumbau Ost« die wohl radikalste Lektion über die Kluft, die zwischen dem Bauen als technisch-funktionaler Dienstleistung und der Schaffung von Lebensqualität für die Bewohner besteht. Damals entwickelte sein Büro das Instrumentarium für grundlegende Modernisierungen und Konversionen von standardisierten und uniformierten Typenhäusern, die sich aufgrund der Starrheit ihrer seriellen Konstruktionen gegen jeden Umbau sperrten. Bei den Eingriffen in die ostdeutschen Plattenbauten musste der Erneuerungseifer des Architekten allerdings die Gewohnheiten der Nutzer berücksichtigen: Viele empfanden das Wohnen im Plattenbau durchaus als Errungenschaft der DDR und Lohn für ihre Lebensleistung. Hinzu kommt, dass sich die Menschen erfahrungsgemäß nicht allein mit ihren Wohnungen, sondern vor allem mit ihrem Quartier identifizieren. Deshalb stand der Architekt vor der Aufgabe, das Wohnumfeld trotz größerer Eingriffe wiedererkennbar zu erhalten.

Haus 07
→ 307

In einem seiner ersten und zugleich spektakulärsten Eingriffe verwandelte Forster von 2002 an im thüringischen Leinefelde eine monotone, 180 Meter lange Plattenbauzeile in eine Perlenkette aus Stadtvillen. Im damaligen Klima der Angst vor »schrumpfenden Städten«[7] hatte der Architekt freie Hand, durch den Rückbau der Obergeschosse und die Entfernung von Zwischensegmenten aus dem unförmigen Bauriegel acht freistehende Einzelhäuser herauszuschälen. So blieben von 150 Kleinwohnungen mit mangelhafter Belichtung, innen liegendem Bad und anonymer Nachbarschaft 64 neue Wohnungen in acht Einzelhäusern übrig, die allesamt über eine Terrasse mit Garten oder geräumige Balkone sowie große Fenster in drei Himmelsrichtungen verfügen.

Der zuvor ungenutzte und ungepflegte Außenraum erlebte gleichsam eine Teilprivatisierung, indem die Flächen vor den Erdgeschossen der Häuser auf Hochparterre-Niveau angehoben und in ebenerdige Gärten verwandelt wurden. Statt der zuvor harten Grenze zwischen innerer Privatsphäre und unstrukturiertem öffentlichem Raum entstanden die Pufferzonen von »grünen Zimmern«, die von den Mietern gepflegt und belebt werden und sich im Laufe der Jahre zu einem gartenstädtischen Ensemble entwickelt haben. Gestalterisch bestand die Logik der Architekten darin, die Zweidimensionalität der dünnen Wand- und Deckenplatten dreidimensional zu transformieren, indem sie die Scheiben zu neuen Volumina zusammensetzten und aus den Konturen und Kubaturen der Häuser, Anbauten und Balkone neue bauplastische Einheiten modellierten. Städtebaulich markiert die Anlage nun den Stadteingang, da eine durchlaufende Erdgeschosswand die Punkthäuser miteinander verbindet und mithin wie eine Stadtkante wirkt.

Platensiedlung
→ sfa.de

Das Gegenmodell zu Teilabriss und Rückbau, wie zuvor in strukturschwachen Regionen geschehen, entsteht seit 2017 im Norden von Frankfurt am Main. Weil die Stadt jährlich um 15.000 Neubürger wächst und heute mit 750.000 Einwohnern die höchste Bevölkerungszahl ihrer Geschichte aufweist, ist der Bedarf an Neubauten und Nachverdichtungen groß. Das bekannteste Vorzeigeprojekt, das ebenfalls das defizitäre Erbe der Nachkriegsmoderne aufwertet, entwickelte Stefan Forsters Büro für die kommunale Wohnungsgesellschaft ABG in der »Platensiedlung«, einem Quartier mit Offizierswohnungen der amerikanischen Streitkräfte aus den 1950er-Jahren. Durch horizontale und vertikale Anbauten und Aufstockungen können die bestehenden 342 Wohnungen erhalten und 684 neu errichtet werden – halb frei finanziert, halb gefördert.

Die Hälfte der Neubauten entsteht in modularen Holzkonstruktionen, die nahezu fertig montiert auf die abgedeckten Dächer gesetzt werden und die Geschosszahl von drei auf fünf erhöhen. Die andere Hälfte der neuen Wohnungen dient zugleich der städtebaulichen Aufwertung. Denn die bislang offene Zeilenbauweise bekommt an den Querseiten neue Kopf- und Brückenbauten, die der zugigen Anlage eine Rahmung und innere Differenzierung geben. So entstehen anstelle der ungerichteten Solitäre künftig großstädtische Blöcke mit definierten öffentlichen Straßenzonen und halb privaten Hofbereichen. Da keine der Versorgungs- und Steigleitungen für die neuen Dachaufbauten durch die Untergeschosse gebohrt, sondern in die Außenfassaden integriert wurden, konnten die Altmieter während des Umbaus in ihren Wohnungen verbleiben. Zudem behalten sie eine sehr handfeste Gewohnheit und bekommen trotz deutlicher Aufwertung ihres Wohnumfeldes keine Mieterhöhung.

Architektur für das kollektive Gedächtnis

Philosophicum
→ 275

Umbauten und Erweiterungen im Nachkriegsbestand stoßen bei Nutzern oft auf weniger Widerstand als bei Denkmalschützern. Das sogenannte *Philosophicum*, entworfen 1958 von Ferdinand Kramer, stand jahrzehntelang im Zentrum des geisteswissenschaftlichen Seminarbetriebs der Frankfurter Goethe-Universität. Sowohl wegen seiner universitären Bedeutung wie auch der Bausubstanz gehört das Haus zum kollektiven Gedächtnis der studentenbewegten

Stadt. Nach dem Umzug der Universität auf das Gelände des IG-Farben-Gebäudes am Grüneburgpark wäre die funktionslose Hochhausscheibe ohne Denkmalschutz wohl abgerissen worden.

Zwar hat Stefan Forster wenig Verständnis für die funktionalistische Architektur- und Stadtauffassung von Ferdinand Kramer, der seine Laufbahn in der Ära des Frankfurter Stadtbaurates Ernst May begann und im Frankfurt der Nachkriegszeit zum leitenden Universitätsarchitekten aufstieg. Dennoch respektierte er Kramers Traditionsort, zu dessen alltäglichen Erkennungszeichen einst auch die verbeulten, überquellenden Aluminiumaschenbecher in den verrauchten Seminarräumen gehörten. In Absprache mit dem Denkmalschutz gelang die Umnutzung in Mikroappartements. Die neue Struktur – 174 Kleinwohnungen im Altbauriegel und 64 in einem parallel davor platzierten Neubau – passt exakt in das Raster des Bestands.

Damals hatte Ferdinand Kramer das Seminargebäude mit einem breiten Grünstreifen von der Gräfstraße abgerückt und auf die Rückseite zum inneren Grünbereich des Campus orientiert. Forster und sein Büro korrigierten dies, indem sie die zuvor ungenutzte Freifläche am Straßenrand mit einem fünfgeschossigen Neubauriegel füllten, der im Erdgeschoss Kita, Café und Gemeinschaftsräume bietet und das Ensemble wieder an die Straße heranholt. Indem der Neubau sich auf die Höhe der benachbarten Blockränder beschränkt, bleibt er zudem deutlich unterhalb von Kramers Altbauscheibe. Auf den ersten Blick erwecken die eng aneinandergerückten Parallelbauten den Eindruck, als würde der neue Trakt die Appartements im Altbau verdecken. In Wahrheit sind die Grundrisse beider Gebäude gespiegelt: Die Wohnungen liegen jeweils an den Außenfassaden, sodass nur die Flure auf den schmalen Innenhof gehen.

Die Struktur der Fassade blieb optisch, nicht aber materiell erhalten. Da die ursprüngliche Stahlskelett-Konstruktion mit ihrem vorgehängten Curtain-Wall zu dünn war, ersetzten Forster und sein Team sie durch eine Stahlrahmenkonstruktion mit eingesetzten, nicht tragenden Leichtmetallpaneelen. Angesichts des Verlustes an Originalsubstanz einigten sich die Beteiligten darauf, im ersten Stock einen »Denkmalflur« mit den Türen, Fenstern und Oberflächen aus dem Ursprungsbau einzurichten.

Lyoner Straße 01
→ 263

Selbst aus völlig eigenschaftslosen Häusern ohne Erinnerungs- oder Denkmalfunktion lassen sich enorme Gebrauchswerte herausarbeiten. So transformierten Stefan Forster und sein Büro in der Lyoner Straße im Frankfurter Bürostadtteil Niederrad 2010 einen gedrungenen Büroturm aus den späten 1960er-Jahren in ein Wohnhochhaus mit 98 Appartements auf 15 Etagen. Die Skelettkonstruktion erlaubte flexible Grundrisse zwischen Einzimmer-Wohnungen und Loft-Etagen. Mit drei zusätzlichen Obergeschossen bekam der plumpe Kubus eine deutlich schlankere Figur, die massiven Betonbrüstungen wurden für einen freieren Ausblick abgesenkt und die Gebäudeecken erhielten offene Loggien. Zuvor schien das Erdgeschoss aufgrund der dunkelbraunen Tarnfarbe der Stützen optisch gar nicht auf dem Boden angekommen, sondern kurioserweise zu schweben; erst durch die weiß verkleideten neuen Stützen im Sockel wurde es geerdet. Insgesamt lässt die klassisch moderne Ausstrahlung des von umlaufenden Fensterbändern und weißen Brüstungen gegliederten Baus an ein mediterranes Strandhotel denken, das nichts mehr von seiner Herkunft aus gestapelten Großraumbüros verrät.

Minimum und Maximum

Gegenüber der Transformation und Modernisierung von Bestandsbauten liegt die Vermutung nahe, dass die Gestaltungsspielräume beim Entwurf neuer Häuser weitaus größer sind. Doch der alltägliche Kostendruck und Regulierungszwang haben dazu geführt, dass die Forderungen nach billigen Materialien und reduzierten Maßen selbst im frei finanzierten Wohnungsbau immer lauter werden. 1936 hatte Ernst Neufert in seiner »Bauentwurfslehre« noch verbindliche Mindestangaben für Bautypen, Grundrisse, Inneneinrichtungen und technische Lösungen beschrieben. Heute scheinen diese Minimalwerte häufig das Maximum im Aufmaß und in der Ausführung von Wohngebäuden anzugeben – bisweilen bewegen sich die Vorgaben sogar noch unterhalb von Neuferts Kanon. So führen die aktuellen Förderrichtlinien im sozialen Wohnungsbau zu immer tieferen Grundstücken, weshalb zur besseren Ausnutzung auch die Grundrisse immer tiefer werden, sodass Bäder und Küchen in die unbelichteten Bereiche rücken. Das ergibt oft Lösungen, die an die Defizite der ostdeutschen Plattenbauwohnungen aus den 1970er-Jahren erinnern.

Die Minimalstandards stammen ursprünglich aus den Forschungen der 1920er-Jahre zum Thema »Die Wohnung für das Existenzminimum«. So groß die Erfolge bei der Grundversorgung der Bevölkerung waren, so wenig Spielraum hatten die Architekten damals hinsichtlich der Wohn- und Lebensqualität. Schon 1938 machte sich der Architekt Fritz Schumacher über die moderne Austerität keine Illusionen und nannte den Wohnungsbau »das unscheinbarste Gebiet des architektonischen Schaffens«. Dabei müssten die Architekten jedoch nicht nur die »Wahrung der Menschenwürde« beachten, sondern auch versuchen, »in die Form der Lösung einen Hauch von Freudigkeit zu bringen«.[8]

Stefan Forsters Büro möchte sich mit dieser Mangelwirtschaft nicht zufriedengeben. Auch wenn Forster seine Architekturentwürfe als anonym, alltäglich, neutral, seriell und dauerhaft beschreibt, wirken sie alles andere als trocken, kalt, streng oder starr. Zwar gehören seine Bauten nicht ins Unterhaltungsfach, doch mit der »Architektur der zusammengebissenen Zähne«[9], wie Wolfgang Pehnt einst den neuen deutschen Konservatismus im Bauen beschrieb, haben sie nichts zu tun. Vielmehr strahlen sie eine urbane Ernsthaftigkeit und zugleich Eleganz aus, die angesichts der reduzierten Billigstandards der Hausaufgabe des Wohnens wieder Respekt erweist und den Bewohnern ihre Würde zurückzugeben versucht.

Zu den Erkennungszeichen von Forsters Häusern gehört, dass sie keine hochgestemmten Skulpturen ohne Sockel sind, die sich zu allen Seiten gleich verhalten und in die Stadt zerfließen, sondern dass sie wieder frontal an der Straße ankommen. Ihre Fassaden bestehen nicht aus spiegelnden Glanzhäuten oder sonstigen körperlosen Membranen, sondern aus verräumlichten Übergangszonen mit starkem Relief und taktiler Stofflichkeit. Ihre Kubaturen laufen in schnellen, abgerundeten Ecken aus und scheinen sich im Stadtraum zu drehen. Die Hauseingänge sind keine Rattenlöcher neben Garageneinfahrten, sondern eröffnen runde Schwellenräume und vertiefte Vestibüle mit Sogwirkung. Es gibt keine auskragenden Vordachkonstruktionen, Lampenhalter, freistehenden Briefkästen oder seitlichen Fallrohre, weil alle Objekte bündig in die Wand eingelassen wurden. Die zumeist durchgesteckten und doppelgeschossigen Entrees sind hell und großzügig, weil sie implizite Visitenkarten der Hausgemeinschaft sind und als Zentren der täglichen Kommunikation dienen.

Die Wohneinheiten sind durch Reserven in Raumhöhe, Grundriss und statischer Belastbarkeit oft reversibel. Zudem lassen sie sich über vorgemauerte Regeldurchbrüche zu Nachbareinheiten erweitern. Drinnen heben die Grundrisse die oft unschöne und auch unsinnige Trennung von Raum- und Erschließungssystem auf, wenn es um Gemeinschaftsflächen geht. Kombinierte Wohn-, Ess- und Kochbereiche ersparen die Platzverschwendung von Speisezimmern, frühere Nasszellen geraten zu miniaturisierten Wellness-Bädern und alle Außengrenzen sind mit Loggien, Balkonen und Dachterrassen zum Himmel hin perforiert. Dabei achten Forster und seine Architekten stets darauf, die herausgestülpte Intimität von Balkonen, die sie für ein Kennzeichen des Siedlungsbaus halten, nur in Innenhöfen vorzusehen; für die öffentliche Straßenseite entwerfen sie ausschließlich Loggien, welche die Privatheit diskret hinter die Fassade zurücknehmen.

Häuser mit Hoffnungen

Forsters Ehrgeiz geht nicht auf das Erfinden von Unikaten, sondern auf das Transformieren von Vorbildern mit Modellcharakter zurück. Seine Referenzen verweisen auf die europäische Architektur der Zwischenkriegszeit, als nicht nur Häuser, sondern auch Hoffnungen gebaut wurden. Dazu gehören die großen deutschen Reformer der 1920er-Jahre wie Hans Poelzig, Bruno Taut, Ernst May, Erich Mendelsohn oder Erwin Gutkind, aber auch die Architekten des »roten« Wiener Gemeindebaus wie Karl Ehn, Karl Schmalhofer, Hubert Gessner, Oskar Strnad oder Josef Frank. Angesichts dieser reichen Wohnungsbaugeschichte mit ihrem Alltagspathos und Formenreichtum verzichtet Forster auf geniale Eingebungen für neue Gestaltungweisen und arbeitet vielmehr daran, solche Ideale in die heutige Realität zu überführen.

Forsters Team greift oft die Tradition expressionistischer Klinkerfassaden auf, aber nicht allein als ausdrucksstarke Schmuckform, sondern auch aufgrund ihrer materiellen Langlebigkeit. Während heutige Wärmedämmfassaden nach kurzer Zeit verschmutzen, erneuert werden müssen und schließlich auf der Sondermülldeponie landen, werden die Fugen bei Klinkerfassaden frühestens nach 80 Jahren erneuert. Weil schöne oder angenehme Häuser weniger schnell abgerissen werden als unansehnliche, hält Stefan Forster die ökologische und ästhetische Nachhaltigkeit für untrennbar.

Westgarten 01
→ 113

Zur Vervollständigung eines aufgesprengten Blockrandes entwarfen Forster und seine Architekten 2005 das Projekt »Westgarten 01« mit 70 Wohnungen an der Frankfurter Speicherstraße, das die gründerzeitlich und industriegeprägte Blockbebauung des Gutleutviertels mit den Solitären des neuen Quartiers am Westhafen verbindet. Trotz ihrer massiven Wirkung besteht die Ziegelfassade zu über fünfzig Prozent aus den Öffnungen der tiefen Loggien und großen, nahezu raumhohen Fensterfronten. Die aufwändige Profilierung des Fassadenaufbaus mit verklinkerten Brüstungsbändern, umlaufenden hellen Gesimsen aus Betonwerkstein und markant abgerundeten Blockecken hebt die Anlage wohltuend von den jüngsten Schlichtbauten im neuen Stadtteil ab. Im Erdgeschoss sichert eine Ladenreihe mitsamt Supermarkt die Nahversorgung im Quartier. Über dem Dach des eingeschossigen Supermarktes im Hof bietet ein hochgelegter, üppig bepflanzter Mietergarten mit Promenaden, Bänken und Wasserbecken eine halb öffentliche Idylle als Bereicherung des geringen Grünanteils im Viertel.

Nicht nur als Blockergänzung, sondern als komplette Hofumbauung entstand 2006 das Sozialbauprojekt in der Voltastraße mit 160 Wohnungen. Obwohl es sich um einen monolithischen Großblock ohne Parzellierung handelt, wurde die U-förmige Anlage in elf zusammenhängende Hauseinheiten mit jeweils 15 Wohnungen unterteilt. Die kraftvolle plastische Gliederung mit klar gesetzten Vor- und Rücksprüngen der Dachlandschaft, negativen Ecken und betonten Fensterlaibungen vermeidet die glatte Lochfassaden-Monotonie üblicher Großblocks. Aufgrund der geringen Deckenhöhe von 2,55 Meter sind die Brüstungen für die stehenden Fensterformate nur 50 Zentimeter hoch; zusätzliches Licht spenden Holztüren mit großen Glasfüllungen. Das gibt es – ebenso wie die 4,50 Meter hohen Foyers in allen Hauseingängen – im geförderten Wohnungsbau nur selten.

Bei nahezu allen Entwürfen Forsters – auch bei dem schneeweißen Schiffsbug des Wohn- und Geschäftshauses »Campus Bockenheim« von 2015, das mit 58 Wohnungen über einer Ladenzone neben der Bockenheimer Warte am Rande der Frankfurter City liegt – fällt ein durchlaufendes Charakteristikum auf: Ob durch farbige Materialwechsel oder wie beim Campus mit monochrom weißen, fast bildhauerisch herausgearbeiteten Verputzsprüngen und Gesimsen weisen alle Häuser horizontal geschichtete Gliederungen auf – eine Gravitationsästhetik, die enorm muskulös und robust wirkt. Diese Häuser heben sich nicht nur wohltuend vom tantenhaften Neo-Klassizismus heutiger Neubauten mit ihren französisch inspirierten Fenstertüren und Grissini-dünnen Laibungen ab, die mangels ausreichender Raumhöhen stets wie Puppenhäuser wirken. Zugleich knüpft Forster mit dem Verzicht auf alle stockwerksübergreifenden, vertikalen Dominanten und Kolossalordnungen auch an die Baukörperauffassung der klassischen Moderne an, die anstelle eines statischen Stilllebens lieber dynamische Beschleunigungseffekte erzeugen wollte. Das nannte Peter Behrens 1914 »das rhythmische Prinzip der Formgestaltung«[10], das den mobilisierten Anschauungsformen der frühen Moderne entsprach, die eine lineare Abwicklung von Fassaden und Straßenräumen favorisierte.

Das bedeutet nicht, dass Forsters Büro dem entfesselten Bewegungs- und Lichtkult im Städtebau nach 1920 anhängt, als Mies van der Rohe oder die Brüder Luckhardt von einer Stadt ohne Steine träumten und ihre Häuser wie gigantische Leitplanken entlang der Asphaltbänder aufstellten. Dafür sind die meist mit dunklem Klinker bzw. rauen Wasserstrichziegeln verkleideten Sockelzonen nicht nervös genug. Mit ihren waagerechten Sägezahn-Reliefs erinnern sie eher an Pressfugen oder Stoßdämpfer. Ebenso lassen sich die horizontalen Profile als Kannelierungen verstehen, die aus der vertikalen Dehnung in die horizontale Stauchung gedreht wurden und latente Rustika-Qualitäten annehmen. Nicht Forsters Häuser sollen fliegen, sondern allenfalls die Blicke und Bewegungen der Betrachter, die sich selbst bei flüchtiger Nebenbei-Wahrnehmung an klaren Richtungen und schnellen Ecken orientieren können.

Reduktion und Ruhe

Ein anderes Entwurfsmotiv zeigt sich in den separat parzellierten Einzelhäusern von Stefan Forster und seinen Architekten: Reduktion und Ruhe. Das Gemeindezentrum des Evangelischen Regionalverbands Frankfurt am Main, das 2012 in der Frankfurter Hafenstraße eröffnet wurde, bezieht seine ästhetische Qualität aus großer formaler Zurückhaltung trotz multifunktionaler Nutzung. Die Kombination aus Kirche, Gemeindezentrum und Altenwohnanlage lässt sich vom Baukörper her gleichermaßen als Blockrand wie als Solitär verstehen, während die verschiedenen Nutzungen ihren Ausdruck in drei unterschiedlichen Fassaden finden: Zur Straßenseite präsentiert sich der Neubau als städtisches Wohnhaus mit Entree, betont durch profilierte Klinkerreihungen als Sockelrelief mit den Panoramafenstern des Gemeindebereichs und den darüberliegenden Fensterbändern der Altenwohnungen mit ihren zurückversetzten Loggien. Auf der Rückseite zum Blockinnenhof öffnet sich die gesamte Fassade mit durchgehenden Loggien, die auf allen Etagen wie Kolonnadengänge ausgebildet sind. Auf der dritten Seite nach Norden liegt ein leicht erhöhter Vorplatz, der zum Entree des Gemeinde- und Kirchensaales führt. Das Flachrelief eines Kreuzes in der Fassade und die turmartige Eckausbildung auf dem Dach stellen eine unaufdringliche Kirchenassoziation her.

Noch stärker reduzierten die Architektinnen und Architekten das gemischte Wohn- und Geschäftshaus mit Kindergarten an der Schloßstraße in Frankfurt-Bockenheim von 2017. Das Ergebnis ist eine geradezu instinktiv wirkende, archaische Typologie. Die Kubatur kombiniert historische und moderne Formen wie Satteldach und Lochfassade, was zugleich eine Anlehnung an die Ästhetik der Primärkörper von Kubus und Dreieck ist, wie sie Aldo Rossi in seiner architektonischen Gedächtnistheorie praktizierte. Die latente alltägliche Wahrnehmungsschwelle wird sogar noch unterlaufen durch die ziegelrote Monochromie des Baukörpers von der Türschwelle bis zur Dachkante, die auch dem zerstreuten Betrachter im Gedächtnis bleibt. Für Forster und seine Architekten ist diese ästhetische Homogenisierung unter anderem auch eine pragmatische Reaktion auf den Wunsch der Bauherren nach Kosteneinsparung. Wo sonst Anschlüsse, Details und Materialwechsel oft mangels handwerklicher Qualität ins Auge fallen, werden unschöne Stellen hier von dem durchgängigen Rot kaschiert.

Die Architektur Stefan Forsters und seines Büros leistet keinen Beitrag zur Lösung der Wohnungsfrage für das Existenzminimum mehr, weil diese historische Notlage im Laufe des 20. Jahrhunderts erfolgreich überwunden wurde. Vielmehr arbeiten die Architekten an der Reformulierung von Ansprüchen an Wohn- und Lebensqualität auf der Basis historischer Wissensbestände und anthropologischer Grundtatsachen. Es geht nicht um Luxuswohnen oder *Loft Living*, sondern um das, was Städte dringend brauchen: Urbanisierung, verstanden als die Schaffung von Zugänglichkeit zu neuen Wohnhäusern und Stadtquartieren, die soziale Teilhabe und kommunikative Verständigung ermöglichen, um den Bewohnern eine Adresse zu geben, an die sie sich gerne gewöhnen.

Die Architektur sei der einzige Bereich menschlicher Tätigkeit, in dem »das erste Bedürfnis und der höchste Zweck so nah verbunden« sind, schrieb Goethe und konstatierte: »Des Menschen Wohnung ist sein halbes Leben.«[11] Wichtigkeit, Beschaffenheit und Ansehen einer Sache bestimmen ihren Wert – und Wert ist nicht nur sprachgeschichtlich, sondern auch ethisch die Wurzel von Würde. Bei aller Pluralisierung der heutigen Lebensstile hängen die Wertschätzung eines Hauses und das Selbstwertgefühl seiner Bewohner nicht allein davon ab, ob ihr Habitat alltägliche Lebensbedürfnisse und Gebrauchsroutinen erfüllt, sondern ob dies architektonisch auch in Würde geschieht. Stefan Forster und seinen Architekten gelingt genau das.

---

1 Johann Wolfgang von Goethe, Brief an den Schweizer Maler J. H. Meyer, 30.12.1795, in: Goethe, Briefe, Bd. 2, 1786–1805, München 1988, S. 212.
2 Vgl. Dieter Hoffmann-Axthelm, Das Berliner Stadthaus. Geschichte und Typologie 1200–2010, Berlin 2011, S. 222, 246.
3 Vgl. Walter Benjamin, Das Kunstwerk im Zeitalter seiner technischen Reproduzierbarkeit, in: ders., Gesammelte Schriften, Bd. 1.2, Abhandlungen, Frankfurt am Main 1980, S. 505.
4 »Implizite Wahrnehmungen können also nicht als unwichtige, aussortierte Wahrnehmungen verstanden werden, die keine Aufmerksamkeit verdienen, sondern im Gegenteil als Grundlage für jede bewusste Wahrnehmung und jede höhere kognitive Leistung. (…) Das beständige ›Nebenbei‹ der Wahrnehmung (…) entspricht in besonderer Weise der Architektur, die eine Kunst des ›Nebenbei‹ ist, indem sie zwar den größten Teil unserer gebauten Umgebung bildet, aber in den seltensten Fällen in den Fokus der bewussten Aufmerksamkeit gelangt, sondern eher im alltäglichen Vorbeigehen implizit wahrgenommen wird. Diese Dimension der Wahrnehmung, die nicht auf bewusstes Verstehen und Nachdenken über das Gesehene ausgerichtet ist, wurde jedoch (…) von der Architekturtheorie vernachlässigt.« Aus: Matthias Ballestrem, Nebenbei Raum. Die Bedeutung von Form und Struktur architektonischer Räume für die Mechanismen der impliziten visuellen Raumwahrnehmung, Diss. TU Berlin 2014, S. 234.
5 Vgl. Karolus Heil, Neue Wohnquartiere am Stadtrand, in: Wolfgang Pehnt, Die Stadt in der Bundesrepublik, Stuttgart 1974, S. 197.
6 Hoffmann-Axthelm, Das Berliner Stadthaus, S. 279.
7 So startete die Kulturstiftung des Bundes 2002 das Initiativprojekt »Schrumpfende Städte« über den Abriss von überzähligen Wohnungen und die Aufwertung von Wohnquartieren. Siehe: Philipp Oswalt / Tim Rieniets (Hrsg.), Atlas der schrumpfenden Städte, Ostfildern 2006.
8 Fritz Schumacher, Der Geist der Baukunst, Stuttgart / Berlin 1938, S. 318.
9 Wolfgang Pehnt, Die Regel und die Ausnahme. Essays zu Bauen, Planen und Ähnlichem, Stuttgart 2011, S. 199.
10 Peter Behrens, Einfluss von Zeit- und Raumausnutzung auf moderne Formentwicklung, in: Jahrbuch des Deutschen Werkbundes, Jena 1914, S. 7.
11 Goethe, in: Briefe, Bd. 2, S. 212.

The Dignity of Housing. Residential buildings by Stefan Forster Architekten

Michael Mönninger

"Man's house is half of his life."
(J. W. v. Goethe)[1]

If there was a leitmotif in modern architecture in the 20th century, then it was resolving the housing question. Each successive generation of architects dreamed of grand social-policy feats and, with remarkable pathos, proceeded to design ever more efficient ground plans for houses and apartments. The result was buildings with precisely defined spaces for different activities and specialised layouts intended not only to rationalise the building process but also to regulate user behaviour.[2] After one hundred years of this ergonomically optimised, top-down architecture, the result is disappointing: Many residential estates and new towns – above all in the second half of the 20th century – are turning into highly subsidised repositories of social crisis; the sprawling suburbs with single-family homes are becoming colonies for pensioners. Those who can, aim to live in an "Altbau", or older property.

However pre-1918 residential apartments account for only 20 percent of the total stock of apartments in Germany. So there is significant demand for new housing that both meets the traditional expectations of durability and variety of use, as well as doing justice to today's spectrum of lifestyles. The predictable day-to-day reality of industrial-era Fordism with a regular eight-hour day is just as much defunct as the model of the nuclear family with the husband going out to work to support his stay-at-home wife and two children. This was the framework that gave architectural shape to urban social and housing policy in the 20th century.

Today it's single-person households, single-parent families, first- and second-generation immigrants and dual-income households with or without children that dominate German society. Then there are patchwork families with children from different partners and a growing group of multiple service-providers, who look for studio apartments in the various locations at which they work. Added to this, there is growing demand for accommodation suited to several generations living together, this reflecting the changing demographics of the German Methuselah society. For by 2050 half of all Germans will be over 60 years old, so one solution to many practical day-to-day problems is for the different generations to come together to live.

For architecture this change means that reference can no longer be made to a standardised model of living. Instead the challenge is to cater for a diversity of individual lifestyles and integrated and interactive ways of living. Yet this new plurality and flexibility in the way we live is up against a grotesque rigidity in the type of housing currently on offer.

Perception through habituation

Frankfurt-based architect Stefan Forster would certainly agree with this criticism of today's housing supply yet without demanding that architectural form is abandoned in view of the dissolution of social role models. Not for him the experiments with flexible, interior walls on adaptable ground plans in biomorphous capsules that are suspended in free-standing support structures, reconfigurable for transitory purposes – this he leaves to others. He holds little of the search for target-group-oriented and tailor-made architecture that adapts to all the changing demands and vital functions of the inhabitants – transparent, movable, mutatable. He counters with his view of anonymity, the day-to-day, neutrality, seriality and durability in building. For him a successful building is one that outlives its inhabitants, that is usable by 90 percent of the population and that escapes any straight-jacketing as regards use.

The soberness of the architectural vision pursued by Stefan Forster and his architects is immediately apparent. The buildings are intended to awaken a kind of déjà-vu effect in the observer, an impression that one has seen them somewhere before, without being able to say whether they were built five or fifty years ago. Even those who do not know the references should find them familiar. This fundamental recognition effect goes far beyond the individual approach towards design of an architectural practice. It rests more on the elementary and aesthetic process of habituation, which takes place via our senses, and which is the basis for feeling at home.

That was what Walter Benjamin meant with his observation that architecture is received on two levels: through perception and use, in other words through our senses of vision and touch. Visual perception, such as when we see famous buildings, happens, according to Benjamin, through a process of contemplation for which there is no correspondence on the tactile, practical side of day-to-day architecture; here reception happens rather by means of habit.[3] Benjamin contrasts attentive perceiving through contemplation and consideration with the incidental noticing through habit and distraction, which appeals not so much to the visual sense as to the sense of movement and touch. Tying in with Benjamin's thoughts on a latent effect of architecture, growing out of habituation, is the more recent theory of perception and architecture. This treats the body-related "incidental perception" of built structures as implicit, unconscious interaction between the individual and the environment in which direct perception is always expanded by indirect predictions and memories.[4]

Yet these subliminal qualities of buildings that are revealed in day-to-day routines – with long-term consequences for quality of life – will remain mostly background phenomena, seldom considered in the theory and practice of building. When architects today appeal to memory and recollection, then they don't so much mean appropriation through familiarity and use, but instead avail themselves of the fundus of architectural history. They like to quote historical forms and images which although inviting contemplative consideration are less suited to incidental long-term use with all the senses. Such vedutas can mobilise emotions but not energies.

The shrinking modern home

Stefan Forster and his team also use references from the architectural history of the early modern and the interwar period a hundred years ago. But they go beyond the reproduction of the cube shapes and expressionist surfaces of *Neue Sachlichkeit* to also ask how to correct, today, the errors and aberrations that occurred in housing in the heroic modern era. For with their ideal designs for estates and urban expansion, the proponents of international *Neues Bauen* after the First World War continued the shrinkage of space that homes in the modern era have experienced, leading to a tearing apart of all traditional routines and social interrelationships. First the work disappeared from the home, then all those people were excluded who were not part of the nuclear family – from home helps to grandparents. General purpose rooms gave way to separate living areas – for every function and person. In this way apartments finally developed into miniaturised private islands: intimate, protected and as far removed from the public sphere as possible.

This introversion presented itself towards the outside in the form of anti-urban estates with undifferentiated green spaces and open areas for sanitised leisure use. With the total socialisation of the process of designing and building spaces for living, the satellite towns and high-rise ensembles after the Second World War achieved precisely the opposite: a maximum of privacy. Because, living in their stacks of individual small-family apartments, people were disincentivised to socialise while also feeling overwhelmed by the collective large-scale estate around them. Maximum isolation and at the same time total integration – that was the consensus back then in housing research – left the occupants with a feeling of "exposure and lack of distance", as regards both the architectural and the social environment.[5]

Today's architecture can present no ideal designs to counter the overspecialised superfunctionalism of segregated housing and estate construction. No more will there be fully integrated urban domestic economies with comprehensive economic participation and social cooperation, also because nobody wants to forfeit the indisputable emancipation benefits that were brought by the liberation from old domestic hierarchies and housing dependencies. Nevertheless modern architecture can indeed be capable of historical self-criticism, in order to compile workable housing and urban structures also from the reservoir of history.

Because the vagrant, liquefied living conditions have broken free of their ties to the home, the most important criterion for future urbanity, according to the Berlin urban planner and architectural theorist Dieter Hoffmann-Axthelm, will be "how many functional and social threads a building can re-connect out of today's isolation".[6] Here he describes the challenge to bring back into the residential environment functions that have so far been moved outside it, such as work and local supplies, looking after the young and the old. After a century of socialisation and externalisation of practically all the functions of a home, the issue now is to regain individual responsibility and social autonomy.

Dismantling and extending

In today's residential construction, such qualities are seldom achievable. Yet we should be happy when architects recognise how large the gap is between the historical and theoretical view of what the aims should be and actual building practice. For Stefan Forster the confrontation with "Stadtumbau Ost", the federal and regional programme launched in 2002 to regenerate cities in the east of Germany, was probably the most radical lesson on the gulf that exists between building as a technical and functional service and the creation of quality of life for the occupants. At that time his architectural practice developed a package of measures for fundamental modernisation and conversion of standardised and uniform housing formats that resisted all conversion attempts because of the rigidity of their serial construction. However, for all the eagerness to renew and regenerate the old prefabricated high-rises of East Germany, the architect had to take into account the way the users viewed and used these old buildings: Many saw these high-rises as a real achievement of the GDR, and an apartment in them as just reward for hard work. Also people tended to identify not just with their apartments, but above all with their particular local urban district. The job for the architect was to ensure the new residential environment retained recognisable aspects despite major interventions.

Haus 07
→ 307

In one of his first and at the same time most spectacular projects Forster transformed a monotone, 180-metre long panel-system *Plattenbau* apartment block in Leinefelde in Thuringia into a string of pearls, or villa-like sections. In a climate of fear at the time of "shrinking towns"[7], the architect had a free hand to carve eight free-standing individual buildings out of the unshapely block, through a process of dismantling upper stories and removing intermediate segments. The original 150 small apartments with poor daylighting, windowless bathrooms and an anonymous neighbourhood, were transformed into 64 new apartments in eight separate buildings, all with a terrace with garden or spacious balcony, and large windows bringing light from three directions.

The previously unused and poorly maintained outside space experienced a kind of partial privatisation, achieved by raising the spaces in front of the ground floors of the blocks to create level gardens at mezzanine level. In place of a hard border between the inner private sphere and the unstructured public space, buffer zones of "green rooms" were created which were tended and actively used by the tenants, and which over the years developed into an ensemble with garden-city character. In terms of design the architect's logic was to transform the two-dimensionality of the thin prefabricated panels used for floors and walls into three dimensions, by putting the panels together into new volumes and forming new architectural units from the contours and cubic shapes of the buildings, extensions and balconies. This residential complex is now also a marker standing at the entrance to the town, looking like a border to the urban area thanks to a continuous wall at ground floor level interspersed with individual buildings.

Platensiedlung
→ sfa.de

The counter-model to partial demolition and dismantling, as previously implemented in economically weak regions, has been under construction since 2017 in the north of Frankfurt. With a population standing at the highest in the city's history (750,000) and rising further each year by 15,000, Frankfurt has a pressing need for new housing and for maximising existing potential through increasing density. The most well known model project, one which also upgrades the deficient legacy of post-war modernism, was developed by Stefan Forster's practice for the local authority housing corporation, ABG, in the "Platensiedlung", a 1950s housing estate for officers in the American forces. By adding extensions upwards and outwards, the original 342 apartments were preserved and 684 new ones built – funded half and half by local government and private investors.

Half of the new space is created by modular timber-framed extensions, placed as almost entirely assembled units on top of the uncovered roofs, raising the number of floors from three to five. The other half of the new apartments has the additional function of upgrading the urban environment. This is achieved by adding end sections and crosswise bridges to the previously open-ended linear blocks; this gives a structure and inner differentiation to what was a draughty row arrangement. Effectively this is turning the unaligned solitaires into large urban residential blocks with defined public street areas and semi-private courtyards. As none of the pipework and ducting for the new roof extensions had to be drilled through the floors below, but was integrated into the outer façades instead, the tenants already living in the blocks could remain in their apartments during the construction work. Familiarity and routines are maintained and, at the end of the process, they have a significantly enhanced environment, with no increase in rent.

Architecture for the collective memory

Philosophicum
→ 275

The conversion and extension of post-war buildings often met with less resistance from users than from preservationists. The high-rise tower called the *Philosophicum*, designed in 1958 by Ferdinand Kramer, stood for decades at the heart of the social sciences department at the Goethe University in Frankfurt. It is very much part of the collective memory of the city and its many vociferous students, both because of its importance to the university and its distinctive presence. After the university moved to the old IG Farben site at Grüneburgpark, this tower, stripped of its original function, would no doubt have been demolished, were it not for its listed building status.

Stefan Forster may have little understanding for Ferdinand Kramer's functionalistic view of architecture and the urban environment, Kramer having started his career in the era of Frankfurt's

The Dignity of Housing

City Planning Officer Ernst May and risen to become the leading architect of Frankfurt University in the post-war period. Yet Forster respected Kramer's tradition-laden location, symbolised once also by the battered, overflowing aluminium ashtrays in the smoky seminar rooms. In consultation with the historic buildings department, the Philosophicum was converted into micro-apartments. The new structure – 174 studio apartments in the old high-rise block and 64 in the new building parallel to it in front – fits precisely into the original grid.

Ferdinand Kramer had separated the seminar building from Gräfstraße by means of a wide strip of green, and oriented the rear of the building to the inner green spaces of the campus. Forster and his practice corrected this by filling the previously unused open area by the roadside with a new, five-storey block which accommodates a children's day nursery, café and shared communal rooms on the ground floor; this effectively brings the ensemble back to the street. By limiting the height of the new building to that of the neighbouring city blocks, the new building also remains well below Kramer's high-rise tower. At first glance, the closely spaced parallel buildings give the impression that the new tract would block the view from the studio apartments in the old building. In truth the ground plans of both buildings are mirror images of each other: The apartments are on the outward-facing façades, leaving only the corridors overlooking the narrow interior courtyard.

The structure of the façade was preserved, in terms of visuals if not materials. As the original steel-frame construction with its curtain wall was too thin, Forster and his team replaced it with a steel-frame construction with inset, non-structural lightweight metal panels. In view of the loss of the original substance the parties involved agreed to set up a "historic storey" with the doors, windows and surfaces of the original building.

Lyoner Straße 01
→ 263

Real practical value can be extracted even from buildings without any particular qualities, or with no public memory function or historical significance. In 2010, for example, Stefan Forster and his practice transformed a compact, late 1960s office tower in the commercial district of Niederrad into a residential tower with 98 studio apartments on 15 floors. The skeleton frame enabled flexible ground plans ranging from one-room apartments to loft storeys. By adding three new storeys to the top, the rather clumsy cube was given a much slimmer figure; the solid concrete parapets were lowered to give a better view; and open loggias were created on the corners of the building. Before this, the dark-brown "camouflage" on the columns gave the curious impression that they did not reach the ground, and that the building as a whole was floating. Cladding these columns in white effectively grounded the structure. Overall the classic modern look of the building after transformation, with its bands of windows and white parapets, has the air of a Mediterranean seaside hotel, quite different to its origins as a highrise office tower.

Minimum and maximum

Compared with the transformation and modernisation of existing buildings, one might expect the scope when designing new buildings to be much bigger. Yet regulatory requirements and everyday pressure on costs have led to ever louder demands for cheaper materials and reduced dimensions, even in privately financed residential construction. Back in 1936, in his handbook entitled "Bauentwurfslehre" (Architects' Data), Ernst Neufert set out minimum requirements for building types, floor plans, interior fittings and building systems. Today these minimum values often seem to be quoted as the maximum in the planning and construction of residential buildings – sometimes the requirements even fall below those cited in Neufert's canon. For example, the current guidelines for publicly funded social housing are leading to ever deeper building plots, which in turn leads to deeper floor plans, to make best use of the space, and that means the bathrooms and kitchens are shifted into areas with no natural light. The result is often solutions that echo the deficits of the 1970s panel-built *Plattenbau* blocks in the former East Germany.

The minimum standards come originally from research in the 1920s on the theme of "The apartment for the existential minimum". Contrasting with the successes in meeting the basic needs of the population, was the lack of scope the architects had in terms of improving the quality of living space. As early as 1938 the architect Fritz Schumacher had no illusions about the modern austerity and said that residential construction was "the most unremarkable area in architectural endeavour". Yet those architects were called upon not just to "preserve human dignity" but to also try and "bring a breath of joyfulness through the solutions they propose".[8]

Stefan Forster's practice rejects this pursuit of the lowest common denominator. And although Forster describes his architectural designs as anonymous, everyday, neutral, serial and durable, they look anything but dry, cold, severe and rigid. No, his buildings do not make headlines, but neither do they have anything to do with the "architecture of gritted teeth"[9], as Wolfgang

Pehnt once described the new German conservatism in architecture. Rather they radiate an urban sobriety and also elegance, thus regaining respect for the job of creating housing and giving the occupants back their dignity, against a background of ever lower and cheaper standards.

One of the distinctive qualities of Forster's buildings is that they are not towering sculptures without a base, the same on all sides and dissolving into the city, instead they have returned to face the street. Their façades are not made up of shiny, reflective skins or other formless membranes, but are composed instead of transition zones that have spatial identity, with strong relief and a tactile materiality. Their cubic volumes flow into rapid, rounded corners and seem to rotate in the urban space. The entrances to the blocks are not rat holes next to ramps leading to underground car parks but open, round threshold spaces and deepened vestibules with a welcoming air. There are no projecting canopies, lamp-holders, free-standing letter box units or downpipes on the façades, all these being integrated instead flush into the walls. Most of the bright and spacious entrances areas go right through the building and are double-height, because they have a representative function for the community that lives in the building, and operate as centres for daily communication.

In many cases there are reserves built into room height, floor plans and structural loading which open the way for later changes to the division of space. They can also be extended into adjacent units by opening up walls at predetermined points. Inside the floor plans remove the often rather unattractive and also illogical separation of rooms and interconnecting spaces in communal areas. Combined living, dining and cooking areas remove the waste of space that dining rooms previously represented; wet rooms are turned into miniature wellness areas; and all outer borders are perforated with loggias, balconies and roof terraces, giving a view of the sky. In achieving this, Forster and his architects always pay attention to where they place the outward-facing intimacy that balconies represent – a feature of residential estates in Forster's view: they are always located overlooking inner courtyards. Loggias, which take the private sphere back discreetly behind the façade, are used exclusively on the street-facing side of the building.

Homes with hope

Forster's ambition is founded not on inventing iconic structures but on transforming existing building prototypes which have model character. His references point to the European architecture of the interwar period when building hope was just as important as building housing. Among those references are the great German reformers of the 1920s such as Hans Poelzig, Bruno Taut, Ernst May, Erich Mendelsohn and Erwin Gutkind, as well as the architects of Vienna's "red" municipal housing programme, with names such as Karl Ehn, Karl Schmalhofer, Hubert Gessner, Oskar Strnad and Josef Frank. In view of this rich history in housing construction with its everyday pathos and wealth of forms, Forster forgoes ingenious contributions on new directions in design, preferring instead to work on translating such ideals into today's reality.

Forster's team often takes up the tradition of expressionist clinker façades, not solely as distinctive decorative shapes but also for the longevity of the material. While today's insulated façades become dirty after a short period of time, require renovation and end up on special landfill sites, the joints on clinker façades last for 80 years before they need renewal. For the reason that attractive or congenial buildings tend to avoid demolition for longer than unattractive ones, Stefan Foster believes that environmental compatibility and aesthetics are inseparable when it comes to sustainability.

Westgarten 01
→ 113

In 2005 Forster and his architects embarked upon a project to close a gap in a city block to provide 70 apartments on Speicherstraße in Frankfurt. "Westgarten 01" connects the late 19th/early 20th century city-block structure of Gutleut with the solitaire buildings of the new district of Westhafen. Despite the solid impression of the brick, over fifty percent of the façade is perforated by either deep loggias or extensive glazed façades with large, almost floor-to-ceiling windows. The contouring detail of the façade, with bands of clinker brick parapets, continuous light-coloured cornices of cast concrete and distinctive rounded corners, makes the complex stand out favourably from the recent simpler buildings in the new district. On the ground floor a row of shops with supermarket caters for day-to-day needs. On the roof of the single-storey supermarket in the courtyard is a raised, luxuriously planted tenant garden, with paths, benches and a pond providing an attractive, semi-public oasis in a district that has few green spaces.

Voltastraße residential development
→ 73

In 2006 Forster designed and built a whole new city block – the social housing project on Voltastraße, providing 160 apartments. Although this is a single, large, monolithic city block, the U-shaped complex is subdivided into eleven interconnected units, each with 15 apartments. The strong, sculptural articulation, with clear projections and incisions in the roof line, recessed corners and distinctive deep-set windows, avoids the smooth punctured monotony of conventional large city block developments. A low ceiling height of 2.55 meters allows for only 50-cm high railings in front of the vertical-format windows and additional daylight is brought in via large glazed panels in wooden doors. This, just like the 4.50 metre high foyer in all entrance areas, is only rarely found in publicly funded housing developments.

With almost all of Forster's designs – including the snow-white ship's prow of "Bockenheim Campus" in 2015, a residential complex with 58 apartments above a retail unit next to Bockenheimer Warte at the edge of downtown Frankfurt – one notices a common characteristic. And that is: whether a building has alternating coloured materials or, as with the campus, monochrome white, almost sculpturally worked projections and cornices, all Forster's buildings have horizontal layers of articulation, a gravitational aesthetic that produces a very muscular and robust effect. These buildings offer welcome relief from the almost camp neo-classicism of today's new buildings with their glazed French windows and grissini-thin soffits, which because of inadequate room heights always look like doll's houses. At the same time, by avoiding all dominant vertical elements extending across floors and monumental orders, Forster also takes up the classical modern idea about the building volume as something that preferred to generate dynamic acceleration effects rather than represent a static still life. In 1914 Peter Behrens called this "the rhythmic principle of form design"[10], which corresponded to the mobilised visual forms of the early modern, this favouring a linear development of façades and street spaces.

This does not mean that Forster's office adheres to the unfettered movement and light cult in urban development after 1920, when Mies van der Rohe and the Luckhardt brothers dreamed of a city without stone, placing their buildings along asphalt strips like gigantic crash barriers. For that the base zones clad mostly with dark clinker or rough watermarked brick, are not restless enough. With their horizontal toothed reliefs, they are reminiscent more of compression joints or shock absorbers. Equally the horizontal profiles can be seen as fluting which has been rotated from the vertical extension to compress horizontally instead, taking on latent rusticated qualities. With Forster it is not the buildings that should fly but the glances and movements of the observers who even if only perceiving these structures in passing, nevertheless can quickly orient themselves on their clear lines and sweeping corners.

Simplification and serenity

Another design motif is seen in the individual buildings on separate plots created by Stefan Forster and his architects: simplification and serenity. A community centre for the evangelical regional association of Frankfurt, opened in 2012 on Hafenstraße, draws its aesthetic quality from great formal restraint despite its multifunctional use. A church, a community centre and accommodation for the elderly are all contained in a volume that can be understood as part of a city-block development and as a solitaire building, the three functions being legible on the three different façades. On the street side the building looks like an urban residential building with entrance area, emphasised by a base with profiled rows of clinker, panorama windows on the communal area and above that, the ribbon windows of the accommodation for the elderly with loggias retreating behind the line of the façade. On the rear of the building, facing the inner courtyard of the block, the entire façade opens up with continuous loggias that are formed like colonnaded corridors on all storeys. On the third side, to the north, is a slightly raised forecourt which leads to the entrance to the community centre and church hall. The flat relief of a cross in the façade and the tower-like corner treatment on the roof present an unobtrusive association with the church.

Even greater reduction was demonstrated by the architects in a 2017 project to build a mixed residential and commercial building with children's day-care centre on Schloßstraße in Bockenheim, Frankfurt. The result is an almost instinctive-looking archaic typology. The cuboid shape combines historic and modern forms such as the pitched roof and punctuated façade, which also alludes to the aesthetic of the primary corpus of cube and triangle as practised by Aldo Rossi in his architectural memory theory. The latent everyday perception threshold is even undermined by the brick-red monochrome of the building volume from threshold to roof top, registering in the mind of even the most inattentive observer. For Forster and his architects this aesthetic homogenisation is amongst other things a pragmatic response to the client's wish to save costs. Where otherwise connections, details and material changes would catch the eye if they were inexpertly finished, here the continuous red colour disguises any less attractive places.

The architecture of Stefan Forster and his practice makes no claim to helping solve the housing problem for those on the poverty line, because this historic emergency was successfully mastered during the 20th century. Rather the architects work on reformulating the requirements as regards the quality of our living space on the basis of historical experience and basic anthropological facts. It is not about luxury apartments, or "loft living", but about that which cities urgently need: urbanisation, perceived as the creation of accessibility to new residential buildings and city districts which enable social participation and communicative understanding, in order to give the residents an address which they will enjoy getting to know.

Architecture is the only area of human activity in which "the primary need and the highest purpose are so closely combined", according to Goethe. He asserted: "Man's house is half of his life".[11] How important a thing is, how high its quality and how highly it is regarded all affect its value – and value is also at the root of dignity. For all the multiplicity of lifestyles today, the regard the occupants have for the home in which they live and their own feeling of self-worth are not solely determined by the extent to which that home meets their needs or fits in with their daily routines. Also important is whether its architectural design also has dignity. Stefan Forster and his architects succeed in offering precisely that.

---

1 Johann Wolfgang von Goethe, Letter to the Swiss painter J. H. Meyer, 30.12.1795, in: Goethe, Briefe, vol. 2, 1786–1805, Munich 1988, p. 212.
2 cf. Dieter Hoffmann-Axthelm, Das Berliner Stadthaus. Geschichte und Typologie 1200–2010, Berlin 2011, p. 222, 246.
3 cf. Walter Benjamin, Das Kunstwerk im Zeitalter seiner technischen Reproduzierbarkeit, in: the same, Gesammelte Schriften, vol. 1.2, Abhandlungen, Frankfurt am Main 1980, p. 505.
4 "Implizite Wahrnehmungen können also nicht als unwichtige, aussortierte Wahrnehmungen verstanden werden, die keine Aufmerksamkeit verdienen, sondern im Gegenteil als Grundlage für jede bewusste Wahrnehmung und jede höhere kognitive Leistung. (…) Das beständige ›Nebenbei‹ der Wahrnehmung (…) entspricht in besonderer Weise der Architektur, die eine Kunst des ›Nebenbei‹ ist, indem sie zwar den größten Teil unserer gebauten Umgebung bildet, aber in den seltensten Fällen in den Fokus der bewussten Aufmerksamkeit gelangt, sondern eher im alltäglichen Vorbeigehen implizit wahrgenommen wird. Diese Dimension der Wahrnehmung, die nicht auf bewusstes Verstehen und Nachdenken über das Gesehene ausgerichtet ist, wurde jedoch (…) von der Architekturtheorie vernachlässigt." From: Matthias Ballestrem, Nebenbei Raum. Die Bedeutung von Form und Struktur architektonischer Räume für die Mechanismen der impliziten visuellen Raumwahrnehmung. Diss. TU Berlin 2014, p. 234.
5 cf. Karolus Heil, Neue Wohnquartiere am Stadtrand, in: Wolfgang Pehnt, Die Stadt in der Bundesrepublik, Stuttgart 1974, p. 197.
6 Hoffmann-Axthelm, Das Berliner Stadthaus, p. 279.
7 Thus in 2002 the federal government's Kulturstiftung started the project initiative "Schrumpfende Städte" (Shrinking Cities) about the demolition of many apartments and the upgrading of residential districts. See: Philipp Oswalt / Tim Rieniets (ed.), Atlas der schrumpfenden Städte, Ostfildern 2006.
8 Fritz Schumacher, Der Geist der Baukunst, Stuttgart / Berlin 1938, p. 318.
9 Wolfgang Pehnt, Die Regel und die Ausnahme. Essays zu Bauen, Planen und Ähnlichem, Stuttgart 2011, p. 199.
10 Peter Behrens, Einfluss von Zeit- und Raumausnutzung auf moderne Formentwicklung, in: Jahrbuch des Deutschen Werkbundes, Jena 1914, p. 7.
11 Goethe, in: Briefe, vol. 2, p. 212.

Städtischer Block
City Block

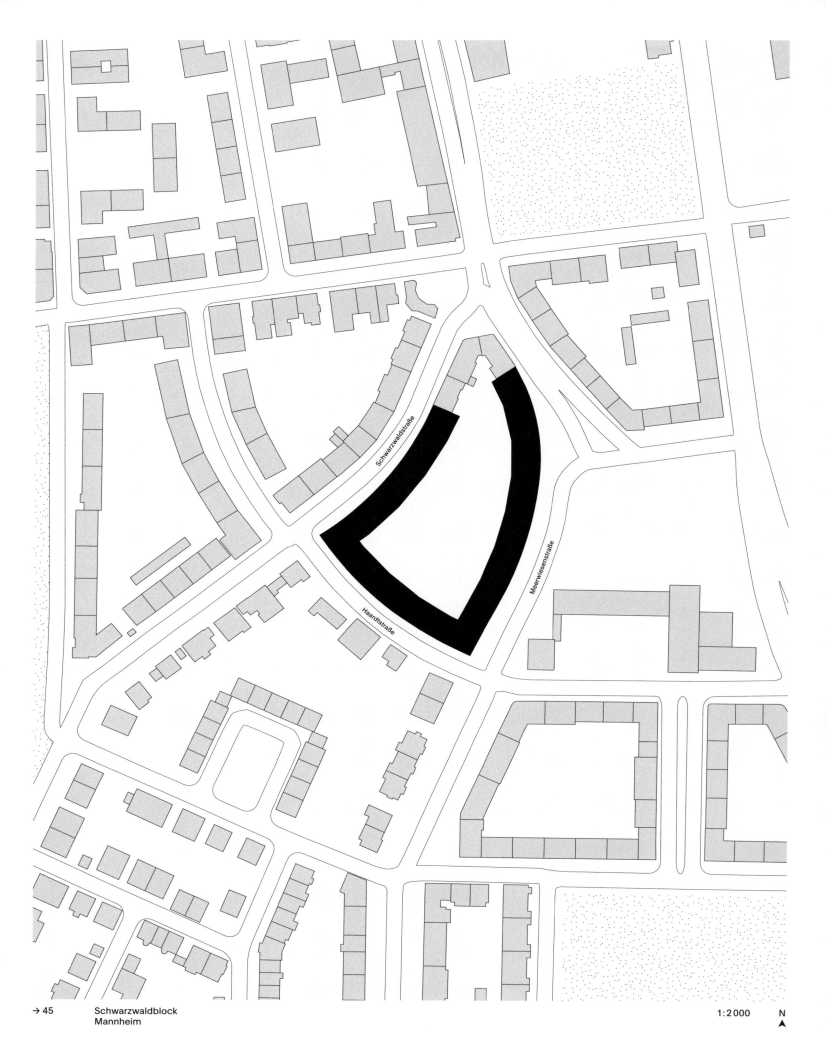

→ 45 Schwarzwaldblock
Mannheim

1:2000

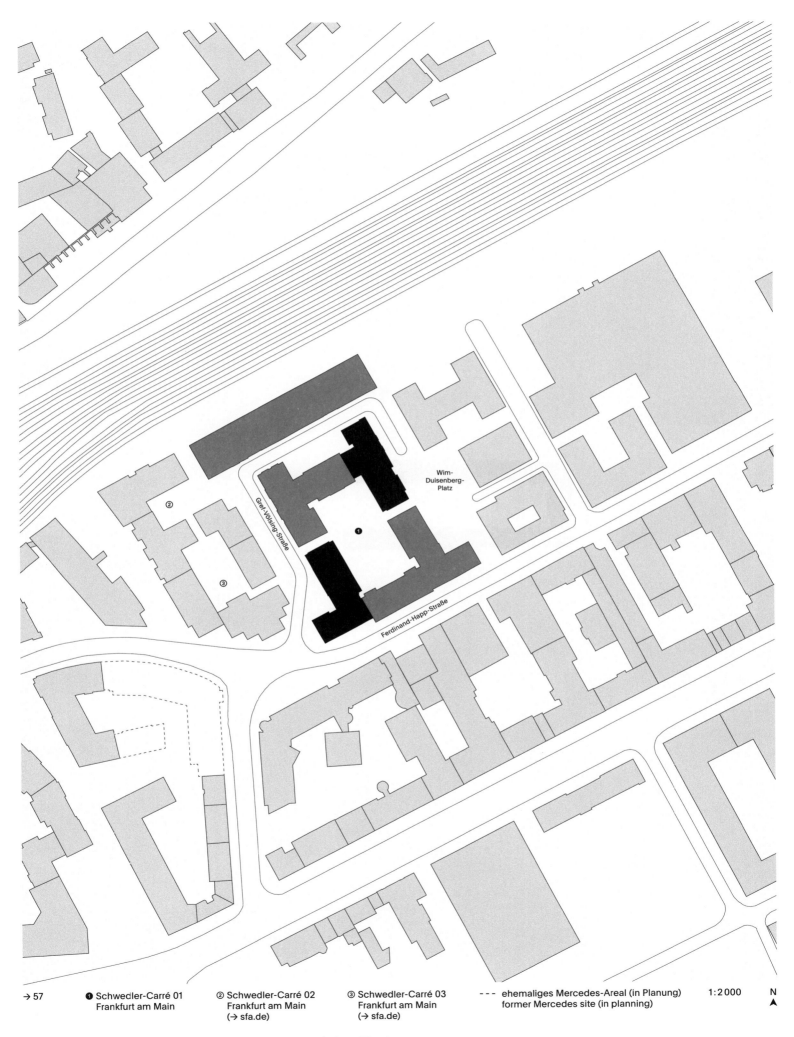

| → 57 | ❶ Schwedler-Carré 01 Frankfurt am Main | ② Schwedler-Carré 02 Frankfurt am Main (→ sfa.de) | ③ Schwedler-Carré 03 Frankfurt am Main (→ sfa.de) | --- ehemaliges Mercedes-Areal (in Planung) former Mercedes site (in planning) | 1:2000 N |

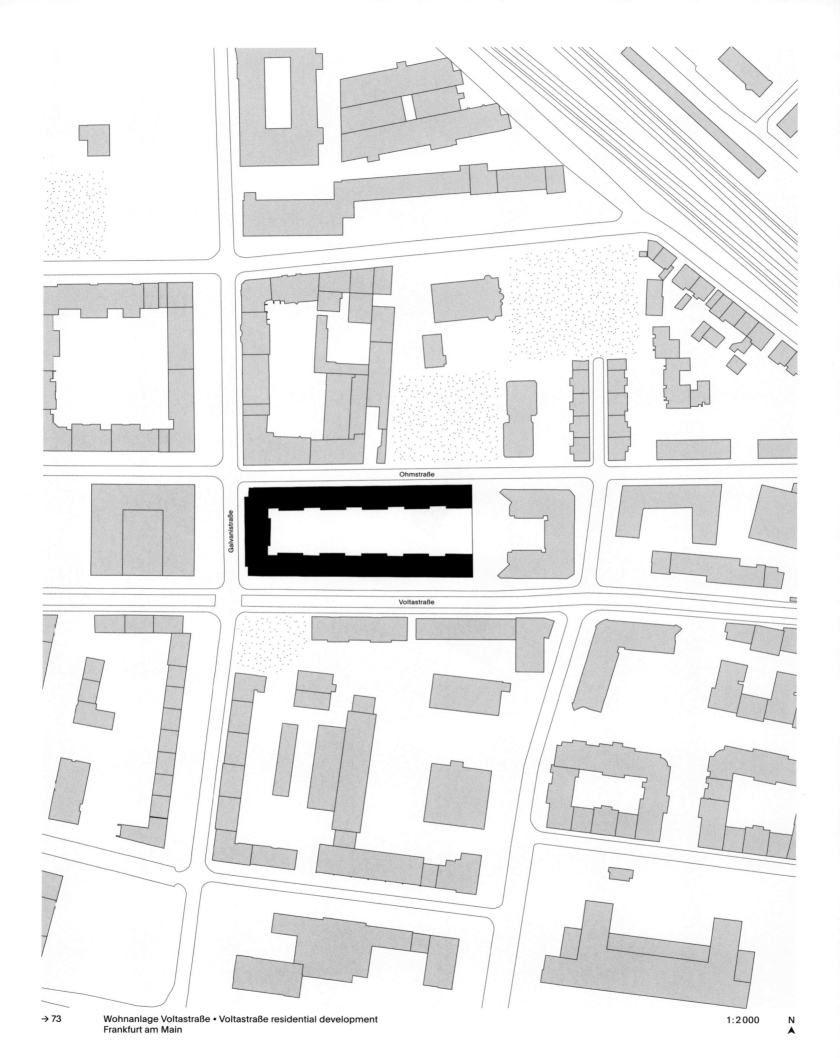

→ 73 Wohnanlage Voltastraße • Voltastraße residential development
Frankfurt am Main

1:2000 N

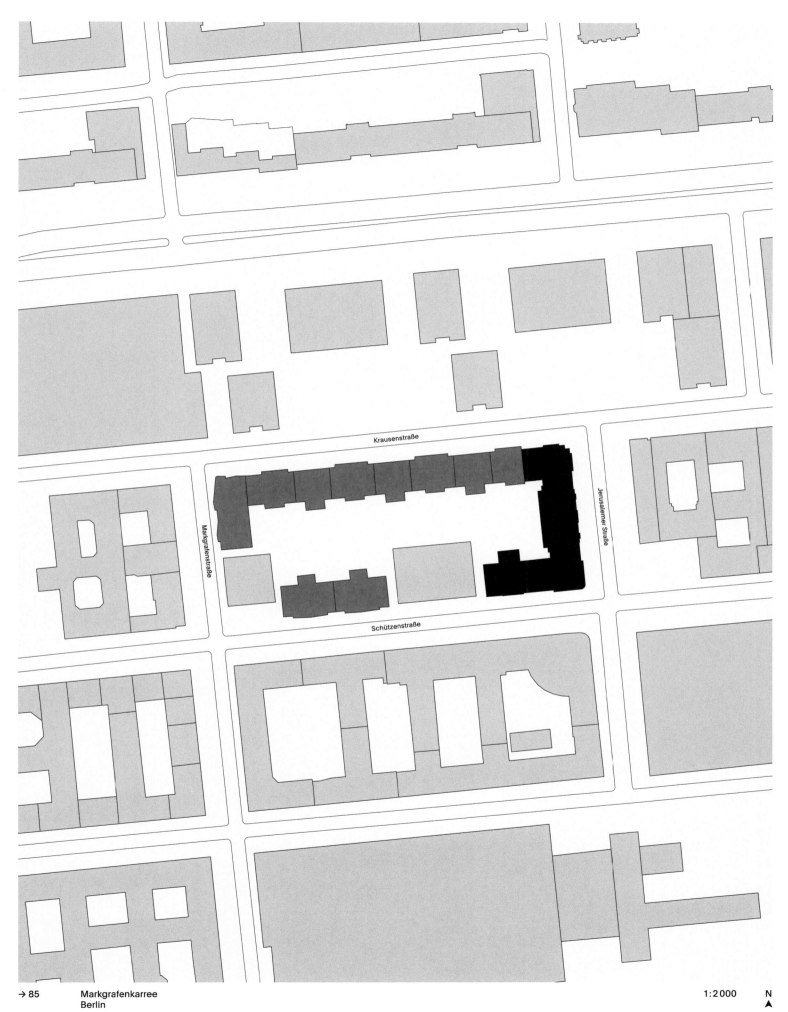

→ 85 Markgrafenkarree
Berlin

1:2000

2007–2016   Schwarzwaldblock
             Mannheim

Der Schwarzwaldblock in Mannheim repräsentiert den Typus des großstädtischen Wohnblocks. Im Verbund mit drei denkmalgeschützten Altbauten, die als solche nicht zum Projekt gehören, bildet dieser einen geschlossenen, nahezu dreieckigen Blockrand, der präzise dem bogenförmigen Verlauf der umgebenden Straßen folgt. Die Geschichte des Areals ist eng mit der des Bauherrn verknüpft, der Wohnungsgenossenschaft Spar- und Bauverein Mannheim 1895: Anfang der 1920er-Jahre erwarb die Genossenschaft das zwischen Schwarzwald-, Hardt- und Meerwiesenstraße gelegene, damals noch unbebaute Grundstück. In den folgenden Jahren, von 1925 bis 1927, errichtete sie dort den Schwarzwaldblock als genossenschaftliche Wohnanlage in städtischer Blockrandbebauung. Nach dessen vollständiger Zerstörung durch Luftangriffe im Zweiten Weltkrieg folgte in der Nachkriegszeit der Wiederaufbau mit aus Trümmerresten gewonnenen, minderwertigen Baumaterialien. Aufgrund irreparabler Baumängel und einer bestehenden Bodenkontamination mussten die 190 Wohnungen des Bestands schließlich zurückgebaut werden. Um die Bewohner im Quartier halten zu können, wurden Abbruch und Neubau zwischen 2007 und 2016 schrittweise in vier Bauphasen realisiert.

Der Neubau des Schwarzwaldblocks zeichnet sich durch einen zeitlosen, unaufgeregten Städtebau aus: Nach außen definiert der fünf- bis sechsgeschossige Baukörper den öffentlichen Straßenraum, nach innen den gemeinschaftlichen Hofraum. Die Großform des Gebäudes, die über den durchlaufenden Klinkersockel und die skulpturale Ausformulierung der Kopfbauten betont wird, steht in der Tradition des Wohnungsbaus der 1920er-Jahre. Inspiriert von den Hamburger Reformblöcken Fritz Schumachers und dem Wiener Gemeindebau schreibt der Schwarzwaldblock die Stadtstruktur in seiner eigenen, klaren Formensprache fort und nimmt das Motiv des unbebauten, kollektiven Hofs auf. Details wie die zu Gesimsen verbundenen Fensterbänke, hellgraue Lisenen, eingeschnittene Eingänge sowie die Materialpalette aus hellen Putzflächen und beigefarbenen Klinkern sind aus den Bauformen der Umgebung abgeleitet. Entstanden sind 235 barrierefreie Wohnungen mit Mietergärten im Erdgeschoss sowie Balkonen und Loggien bzw. Dachterrassen in den Obergeschossen.

Typologically the Schwarzwaldblock in Mannheim is an urban residential block. In combination with three older buildings with listed status that do not form part of the project, this block forms a closed, almost triangular perimeter development which precisely follows the arc of the surrounding streets. The history of this site is closely connected with the site owner – a housing cooperative called *Wohnungsgenossenschaft Spar- und Bauverein Mannheim 1895*. In the early 1920s the cooperative acquired the undeveloped plot between Schwarzwaldstraße, Hardtstraße and Meerwiesenstraße. In the following years, from 1925 to 1927, it then built the Schwarzwaldblock, a cooperative housing complex, laid out as an urban perimeter-block development. The housing was completely destroyed in air raids in the Second World War, and subsequently rebuilt using low-quality building materials salvaged from the rubble. Because of irreparable building defects and the contaminated soil at the site, it became necessary to demolish the 190 apartments in this rebuilt complex. In order to be able to keep the residents in the district, demolition work and the construction of the new housing development was conducted step by step, in four phases between 2007 and 2016.

The new Schwarzwaldblock is an example of timeless, quiet urban architecture: Towards the outside the five- to six-storey building volume defines the street space, on the inside it encloses a shared courtyard area. The overall shape of the development, with its continuous clinker-clad base storey and sculpted corner buildings, follows the tradition of residential housing design of the 1920s. Inspired by the "reform blocks" of Fritz Schumacher in Hamburg and the social housing tradition in Vienna, the Schwarzwaldblock continues the urban structure in its own, clear language of forms and takes up the motif of the open courtyard for collective use. The building forms encountered in surrounding development influenced the design of details such as the window ledges combining to create cornices, the light-grey pilaster strips and the incised entrance areas, as well as the palette of materials with light-coloured plaster surfaces and beige-coloured clinker bricks. In total the Schwarzwaldblock provides 235 barrier-free apartments with tenant gardens on the ground floor, and balconies and loggias, or roof terraces, for the apartments above.

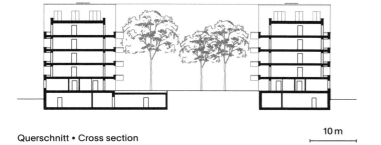

Querschnitt • Cross section — 10 m

Wohnungen • Apartments: 235
Geschossfläche (BGF) • Floor area (gross): 26 030 m²
Fertigstellung • Completion: 2007–2016
Bauherr • Client: Baugenossenschaft Spar- und Bauverein 1895 Mannheim eG
Mitarbeit • Project team: Florian Kraft, Jelena Duchrow, Ildikó Návay, Ferdinand Oswald, Andreas Wenger
Adresse • Address: Schwarzwaldstraße 5–13, Haardtstraße 15–19, Meerwiesenstraße 4–18, 68163 Mannheim

← Blick von Süden auf die Ecke Haardtstraße / Meerwiesenstraße • View from the south, junction of Haardtstraße / Meerwiesenstraße
→ Blick in die Schwarzwaldstraße / Ecke Haardtstraße • Junction of Schwarzwaldstraße / Haardtstraße

Fassadenansicht an der Schwarzwaldstraße mit anschließendem Altbau (links)
Façade elevation, Schwarzwaldstraße with adjacent existing building (left)

Grundriss Regelgeschoss • Standard floor plan

Schwarzwaldblock

← Blick über den Hof nach Südwesten • View across the courtyard towards the southwest
→ Fassadenprofilierung an der Schwarzwaldstraße • Façade modulation on Schwarzwaldstraße

Vorgartenzone entlang der Haardtstraße • Front garden zone along Haardtstraße

← Gref-Völsing-Straße 4 und 6 am südlichen Quartierseingang • Gref-Völsing-Straße 4 and 6 at the southern entrance to the development
→ Ostseite des Carrés am Wim-Duisenberg-Platz • East side of the Carré on Wim-Duisenberg-Platz

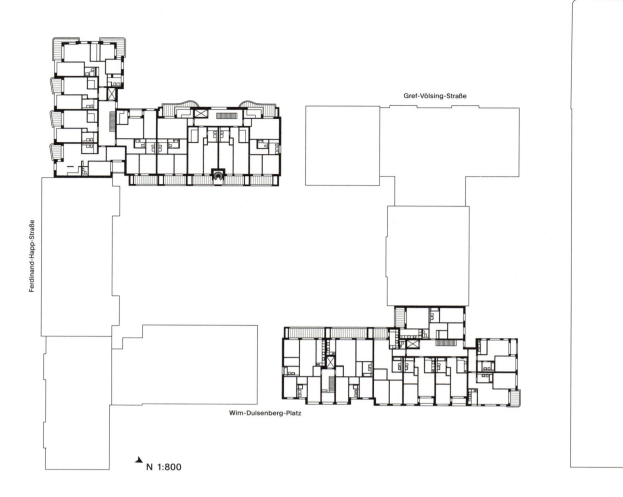
Grundriss Regelgeschoss • Standard floor plan

Blick von Norden in den verkehrsberuhigten Innenbereich • View from the north into the traffic-calmed central area

Schwedler-Carré 01

← Blick über den Wim-Duisenberg-Platz mit den Gebäuden von *Karl Dudler Architekten* (links) und *Ortner & Ortner Baukunst* (Klinkergebäude im Hintergrund)
View across Wim-Duisenberg-Platz with the buildings by *Karl Dudler Architekten* (left) and *Ortner & Ortner Baukunst* (clinker building in the background)
↓ Fassadendetails der Gref-Völsing-Straße 6 • Façade details, Gref-Völsing-Straße 6

Fassade entlang der Ferdinand-Happ-Straße (rechts der Bauteil von *Ortner & Ortner Baukunst*) • Façade along Ferdinand-Happ-Straße (to the right, the section by *Ortner & Ortner Baukunst*)

← Blick von Norden in den Innenhof (rechts der Bauteil von *Karl Dudler Architekten*) • View across the inner courtyard from the north (to the right the section by *Karl Dudler Architekten*)
→ Hauseingang am Wim-Duisenberg-Platz • Building entrance on Wim-Duisenberg-Platz

Fassadendetails in der Ferdinand-Happ-Straße • Façade details on Ferdinand-Happ-Straße

← Fassadenansicht an der Ecke Galvanistraße / Voltastraße • Façade elevation at the junction of Galvanistraße / Voltastraße
→ Blick nach Westen in die Ohmstraße / Ecke Galvanistraße • View towards the west down Ohmstraße / junction of Galvanistraße

Fassadendetails in der Voltastraße • Façade details on Voltastraße

Fassadenprofilierung und Hauseingang in der Ohmstraße • Façade modulation and building entrance on Ohmstraße

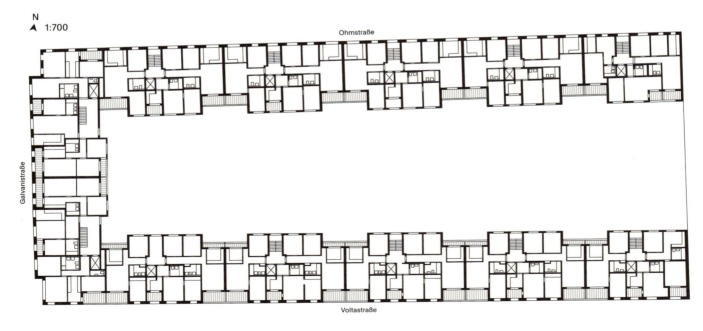

← Blick in den Hof nach Westen • View across the courtyard towards the west
→ Grundriss Regelgeschoss • Standard floor plan

Städtischer Block • City Block

Fassadenausbildung an der Ecke Ohmstraße / Galvanistraße • Façade details, junction of Ohmstraße / Galvanistraße

Blick von Nordosten auf die Ecke Jerusalemer Straße / Krausenstraße • View from the northeast, junction of Jerusalemer Straße / Krausenstraße

Fassadenansicht Schützenstraße / Ecke Jerusalemer Straße • Façade elevation, Schützenstraße / junction of Jerusalemer Straße

Ostseite des Gebäudes an der Jerusalemer Straße (im Hintergrund der »Komplex Leipziger Straße«)
East side of the building on Jerusalemer Straße (in the background the Leipziger Straße complex)

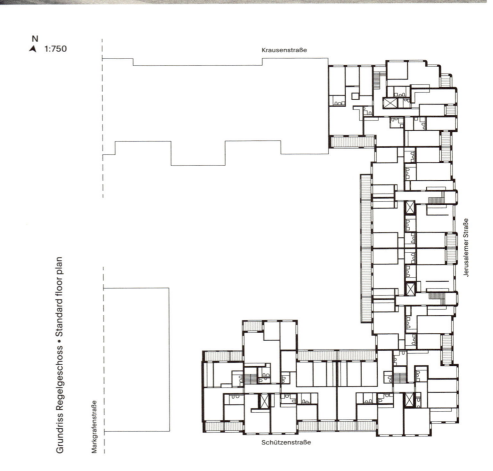

Grundriss Regelgeschoss • Standard floor plan

Städtischer Block • City Block

Fassadenausbildung an der Jerusalemer Straße • Façade details on Jerusalemer Straße

Haus in der Stadt
City Building

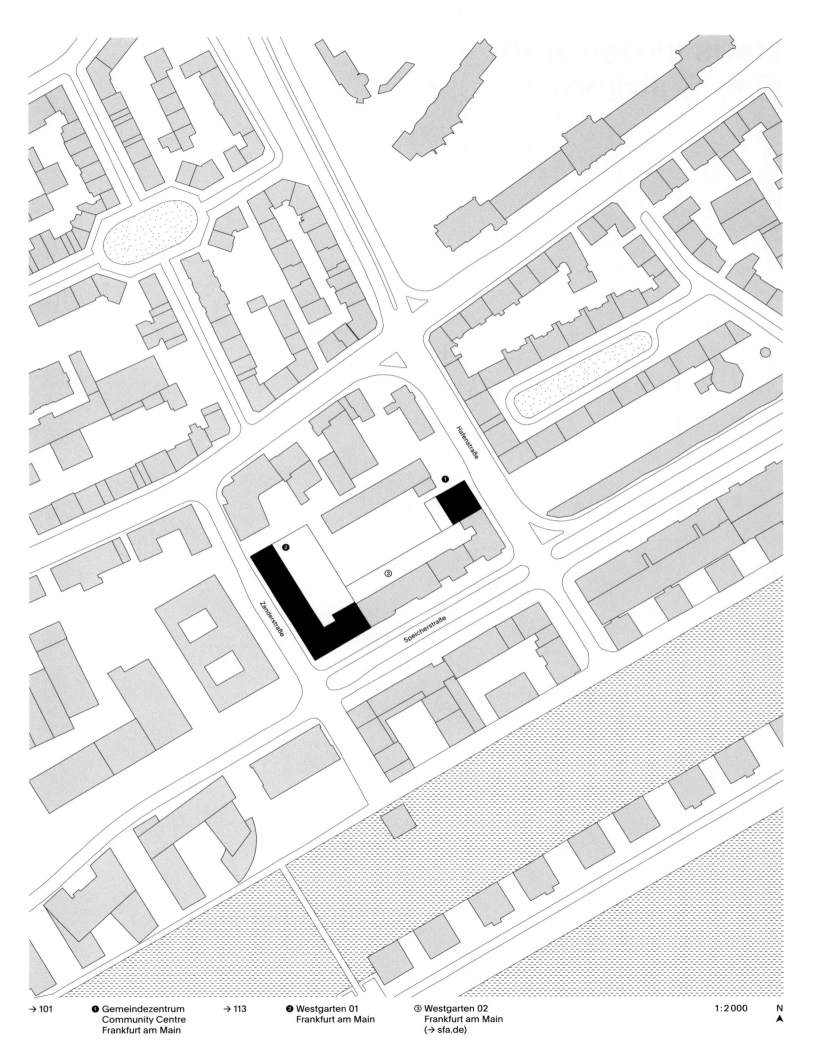

→ 101　❶ Gemeindezentrum
　　　　Community Centre
　　　　Frankfurt am Main

→ 113　❷ Westgarten 01
　　　　Frankfurt am Main

　　　　❸ Westgarten 02
　　　　Frankfurt am Main
　　　　(→ sfa.de)

1:2000　N

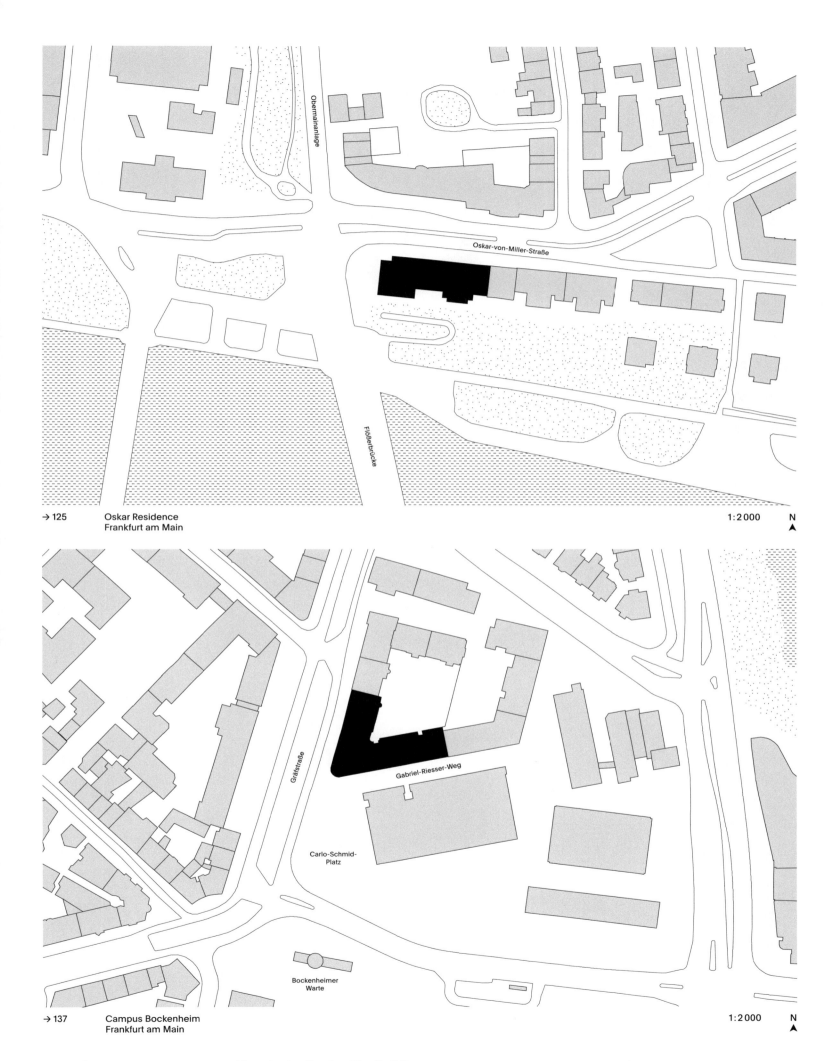

→ 125 Oskar Residence
Frankfurt am Main

1:2000 N

→ 137 Campus Bockenheim
Frankfurt am Main

1:2000 N

Haus in der Stadt • City Building

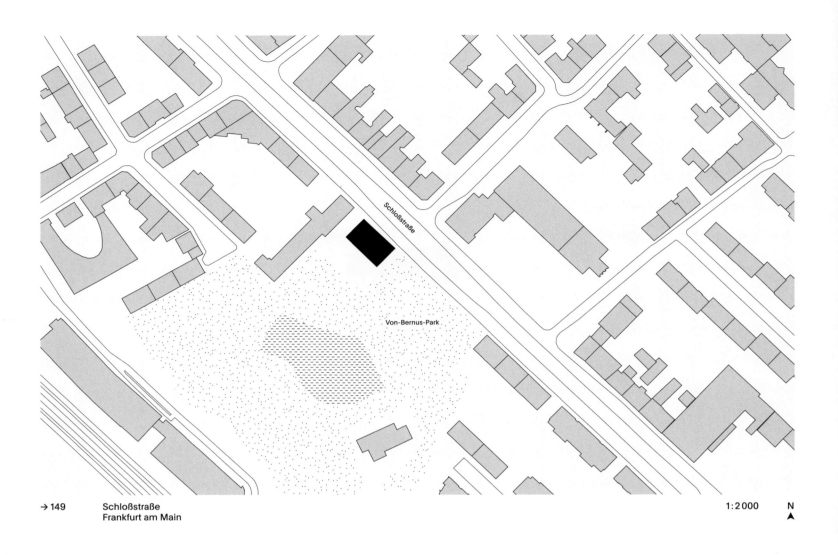

→ 149 Schloßstraße
Frankfurt am Main

1:2000 N

96 Lagepläne • Site plans

→ 161 ❶ Sandweg
Frankfurt am Main

→ 169 ❷ Wohnen auf Naxos
Living on Naxos
Frankfurt am Main

1:2 000   N

Haus in der Stadt • City Building

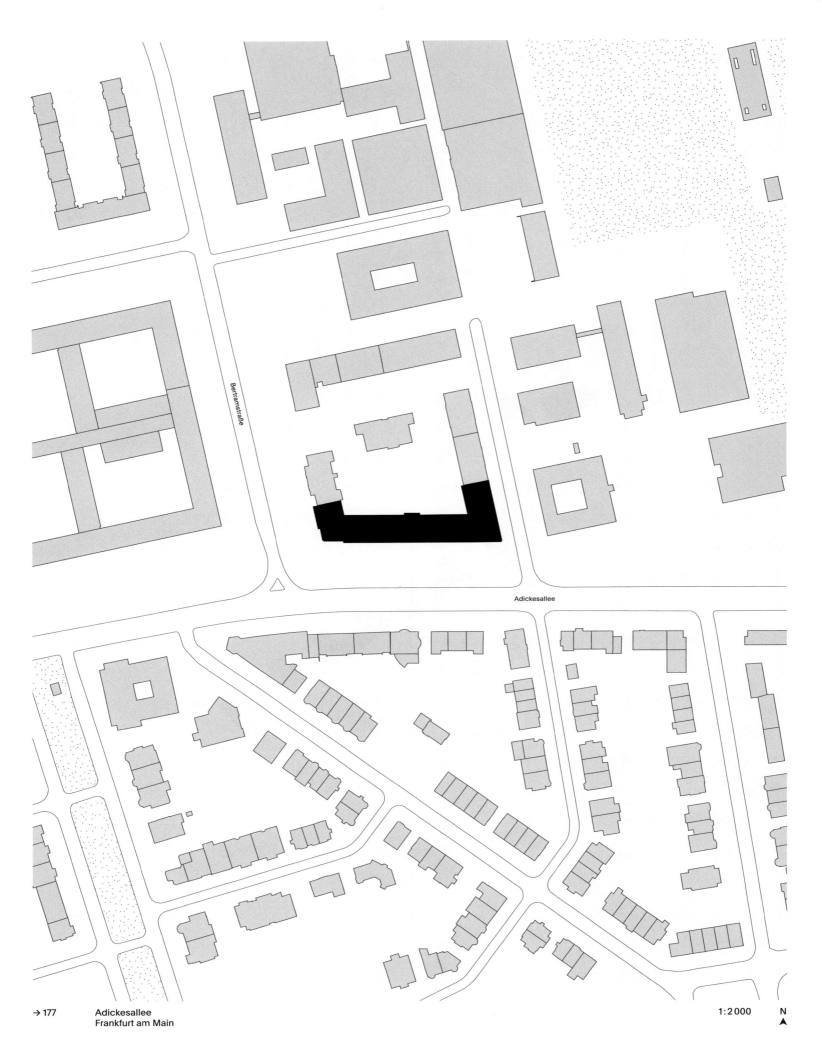

→ 177 Adickesallee
Frankfurt am Main

1:2000

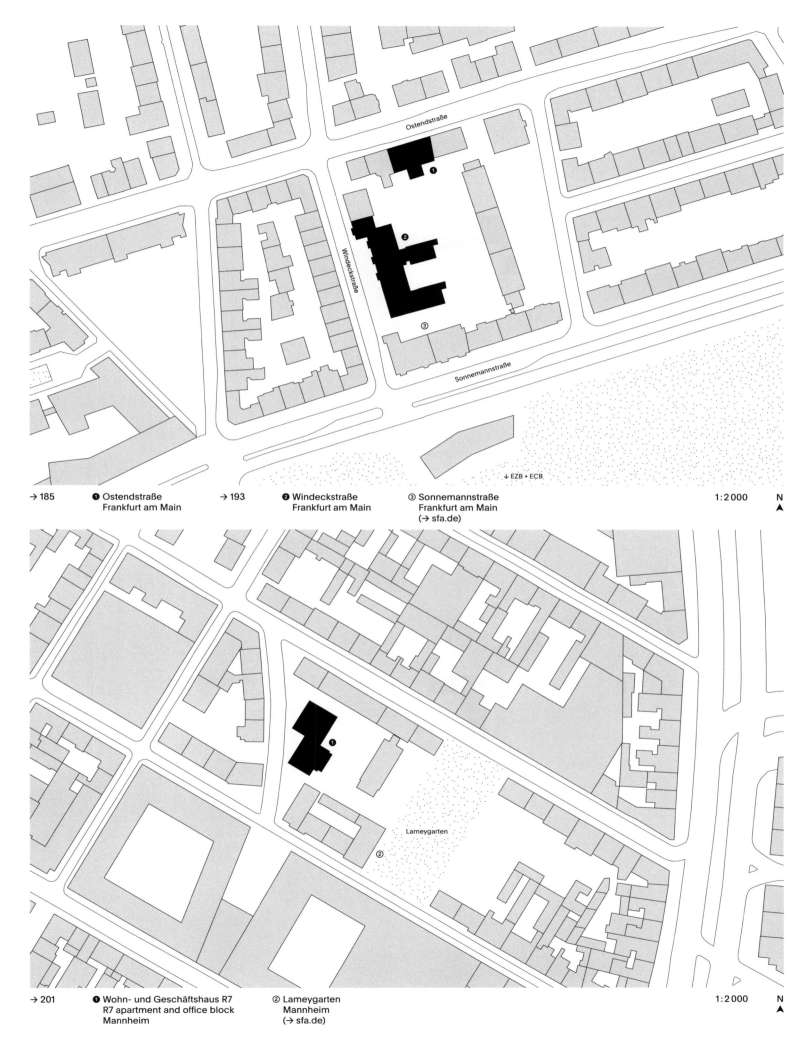

→ 185　❶ Ostendstraße
　　　　　Frankfurt am Main

→ 193　❷ Windeckstraße
　　　　　Frankfurt am Main

　　　　　③ Sonnemannstraße
　　　　　Frankfurt am Main
　　　　　(→ sfa.de)

1:2000　N

→ 201　❶ Wohn- und Geschäftshaus R7
　　　　　R7 apartment and office block
　　　　　Mannheim

　　　　　② Lameygarten
　　　　　Mannheim
　　　　　(→ sfa.de)

1:2000　N

Haus in der Stadt • City Building

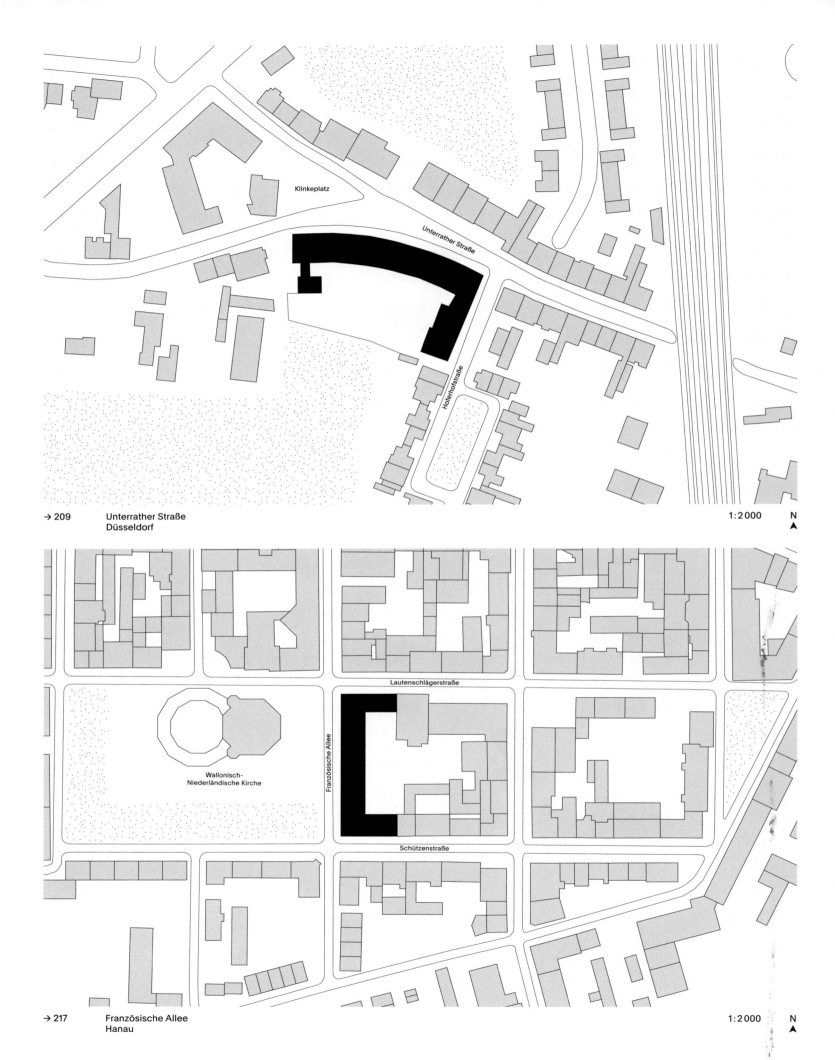

→ 209　Unterrather Straße
　　　　Düsseldorf　　　　　　　　　　　　　　　　1:2000

→ 217　Französische Allee
　　　　Hanau　　　　　　　　　　　　　　　　　　1:2000

100　　　　Lagepläne • Site plans

Blick von Nordosten auf das Gemeindezentrum mit Vorplatz (rechts im Bild) • View from the northeast of the community centre and forecourt (right in picture)

Haus in der Stadt • City Building

Ostseite des Gebäudes an der Hafenstraße mit Eingang zum Wohntrakt • East side of the building on Hafenstraße with entrance to residential section

← Eingangsbereich des Gemeindezentrums mit reliefiertem Kreuz • Entrance to the community centre with relief cross
↓ Blick von Norden über den Vorplatz mit Eingang zum Gemeindezentrum • View from the north of the courtyard with entrance to community centre

Haus in der Stadt • City Building

Blick auf die Westseite des Gebäudes mit Loggien (vom Wohnhaus »Westgarten 01«) • View of the west side of the building with loggias (viewed from "Westgarten 01" apartment block)

Gemeindesaal mit Eingängen • Community hall with entrances

Grundriss Regelgeschoss • Standard floor plan

N ◀ 1:250

Haus in der Stadt • City Building

Eingangsbereich und Treppenaufgang im Wohntrakt • Entrance area and stairs, residential section

← Speicherstraße am Abend mit anschließendem Wohnhaus »Westgarten 02« (2013) • Speicherstraße in the evening, with adjacent Westgarten 02 apartment block (2013)
→ Blick von Süden auf die Ecke Zanderstraße / Speicherstraße • View from the south of the junction of Zanderstraße / Speicherstraße

Eingangsbereich mit Treppenaufgang zum Garten • Entrance area with stairs up to the garden

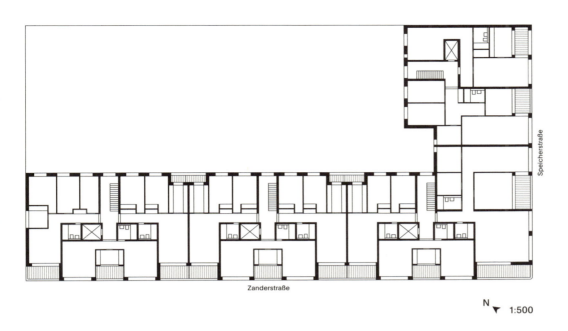

Grundriss Regelgeschoss • Standard floor plan

Speicherstraße

Zanderstraße

N 1:500

Blick über den Garten nach Süden • View over the garden towards the south

Haus in der Stadt • City Building

Loggien an der Ecke Zanderstraße / Speicherstraße • Loggias at the junction of Zanderstraße / Speicherstraße

Haseingang in der Zanderstraße • Entrance to the building on Zanderstraße

Fassadenansicht an der Ecke Zanderstraße / Speicherstraße • Façade elevation at the junction of Zanderstraße / Speicherstraße

2017 Oskar Residence
Frankfurt am Main

Anfang der 1970er-Jahre schaltete Dieter Engel eine Zeitungsannonce: »Suche in sozial schwachen Gebieten Fläche, die sich über Jahre schlecht vermieten lässt.« Fündig wurde er schließlich in der Oskar-von-Miller-Straße im damals noch stark industriell geprägten Frankfurter Ostend. Hier standen nicht nur etliche Häuser leer, sondern im einstigen Toleranzgebiet wurde auch Prostitution geduldet, sodass Engel mit dem »Sudfass« jenes Bordell eröffnen konnte, das später stadtbekannt werden sollte. Begünstigt durch die dynamische Entwicklung des Ostends, dass sich mehr und mehr zu einem attraktiven Kreativ- und Wohnbezirk entwickelte, wurden die vier Bestandshäuser des Sudfass' nach über vierzig Jahren Betrieb 2013 an den Frankfurter Projektentwickler Oskar Grundbesitz GmbH verkauft. Der neue Eigentümer beauftragte nach einem gewonnenen Gutachterverfahren *Stefan Forster Architekten* mit der Planung von zwei Neubauten, die als Boarding- bzw. Wohnhaus dienen sollten.

Die Lage des Grundstücks bot die einmalige Chance, ein innenstadtnahes Wohnprojekt in direkter Beziehung zum Main neu zu entwickeln. Zwischen Straße und Mainufer setzt die »Oskar Residence« die bestehende Häuserzeile fort. Die städtebaulich exponierte Ecksituation wird durch einen zehngeschossigen Turm gebildet, der das Boardinghaus mit 70 *Serviced Apartments* aufnimmt, während ein niedrigerer Seitenflügel zum achtgeschossigen, in hellem Klinker ausgeführten Nachbarhaus mit 28 Eigentumswohnungen vermittelt. Der knapp 30 Meter hohe, in erdigem Rot gehaltene Turm markiert die Schnittstelle von Innenstadt und Ostend: Aus westlicher Richtung bildet er mit dem gegenüberliegenden Eckgebäude eine Art Tor zum Ostend, zusätzlich betont durch das Doppelhochhaus der Europäischen Zentralbank (2014) in der Straßenflucht. Von Süden her markiert er den Eingang in die Wallanlagen, die als ringförmige Grünanlage die Innenstadt umgeben. Mit seiner hochwertigen, dezent ornamentierten Klinkerfassade nimmt die »Oskar Residence« Bezug auf die industrielle Tradition des Ostends. Während die drei Hauptfassaden des Turms durch große, liegende Öffnungen gegliedert sind, dominieren beim Wohnhaus stehende Fensterformate und symmetrisch aufgebaute Mittelrisalite. Jede Wohnung ist nach Süden zum Main hin orientiert und mit großzügigen Freibereichen in Form von Privatgärten, Loggien und Dachterrassen ausgestattet.

Im Rahmen des Projekts wurde der öffentliche Raum zwischen »Oskar Residence«, Flößerbrücke und Mainufer neu gestaltet und eine direkte Verbindung zur Uferpromenade geschaffen.

At the beginning of the 1970s, a certain Dieter Engel placed an ad in a local newspaper: "Wanted: Properties in socially disadvantaged areas that have been hard to let for years." In the end he found what he was looking for in Oskar-von-Miller Straße in what was then a very industrial area in Frankfurt´s Ostend. Many buildings there had stood empty for years, and it was an area in which prostitution was tolerated by the authorities. In fact Engel was able to open a brothel here, the "Sudfass", which became well known throughout the city. Prompted by the dynamic development of the Ostend, which steadily grew into an attractive residential and creative district, the four buildings that made up the Sudfass were sold in 2013, after forty years in business, to the Frankfurt project developer Oskar Grundbesitz GmbH. Following an expert opinion procedure won by *Stefan Forster Architekten*, the new owner commissioned Forster to design two new buildings – a serviced apartment building, and an apartment block.

Because of its location, the plot offered a unique opportunity to build a new-style residential project, close to the city centre and right by the River Main. Between the street and the banks of the Main, the "Oskar Residence" continues the line of the existing development. This prominent corner situation is marked by a ten-storey tower which contains 70 serviced apartments. A lower side section links this corner tower to the eight-floor apartment block in light clinker brick, with 28 freehold apartments. The almost 30-metre high, earth-red coloured tower marks the interface between the inner city and the Ostend district: From the west it is seen as part of a gateway-like situation in conjunction with the corner building opposite, given added emphasis by the double high-rise of the European Central Bank headquarters (2014) further down the street. From the south, the tower marks the entrance to the embankments, an area of green encircling the inner city. With its high-quality, subtly ornamented clinker façade, the "Oskar Residence" takes its reference from the industrial tradition of the Ostend. While the three main façades of the tower are articulated with large, horizontal-format openings, the apartment block has vertical-format windows and a symmetrical alignment of the projecting and receding sections on the façade. Each apartment is oriented towards the south, to the river, and has generously sized outdoor spaces in the form of private gardens, loggias or roof terraces.

As part of the project, the public space between the "Oskar Residence", Flößerbrücke and the banks of the river Main are to be redesigned to create a direct connection to the riverside promenade.

Querschnitt Wohnhaus mit Ansicht Appartementhaus • Cross section of residential block with elevation of tower

Programm • Scope: 28 Wohnungen, 70 Appartements, Gastronomie • 28 freehold apartments, 70 serviced apartments, gastronomy
Geschossfläche (BGF) • Floor area (gross): 8 810 m^2
Fertigstellung • Completion: 2017
Bauherr • Client: Oskar Grundbesitz GmbH & Co. KG
Mitarbeit • Project team: Axel Hess, Jelena Duchrow, María Aparicio Álvarez, Moritz Kaiser, Zoltan Lepenye
Adresse • Address: Oskar-von-Miller-Straße 10–12, 60314 Frankfurt am Main

← Mainpanorama von Süden mit Flößerbrücke und Skyline • Panorama of the river Main from the south with Flößerbrücke and skyline
→ Nordseite des Appartementhauses an der Oskar-von-Miller-Straße • North side of the serviced apartment block on Oskar-von-Miller-Straße

Blick nach Südosten über die Obermainanlage • View towards the southeast across the Obermainanlage

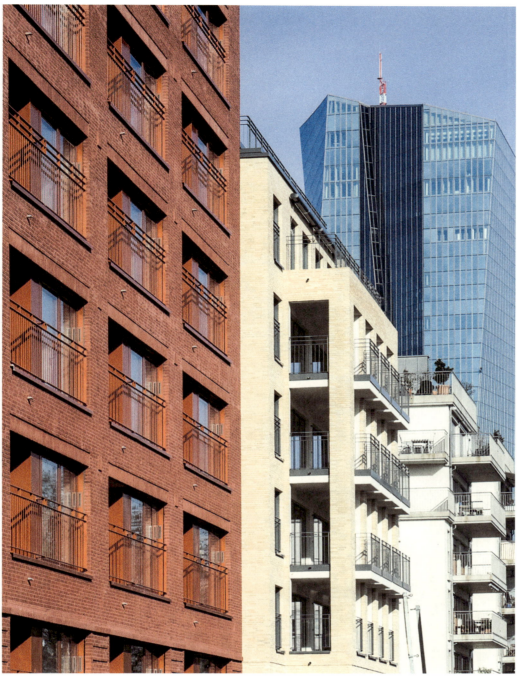

Blick nach Westen entlang der Südfassade (im Hintergrund die Europäische Zentralbank)
View towards the west along the south façade (in the background the European Central Bank)

← Blick nach Süden auf die Kreuzung Oskar-von-Miller-Straße / Flößerbrücke (im Hintergrund das Hochhaus »Mainplaza« von Hans Kollhoff)
View towards the south, junction of Oskar-von-Miller-Straße / Flößerbrücke (in the background, the Mainplaza high-rise by Hans Kollhoff)

Grundriss Regelgeschoss · Standard floor plan

Haus in der Stadt · City Building

Fassadendetails an der Nordwestecke des Appartementhauses • Façade details on the northwest corner of the serviced apartment building

2015　Campus Bockenheim
　　　Frankfurt am Main

Seit seiner Gründung im Jahr 1914 bildete der Campus Bockenheim fast hundert Jahre lang den Hauptstandort der Frankfurter Goethe-Universität. Mit dem Umzug der geistes- und naturwissenschaftlichen Fakultäten ins Westend und an den Riedberg wird der alte Campus bis 2022 schrittweise aufgegeben. Hierdurch bot sich bereits zu Beginn der 2000er-Jahre die Chance, ein neues Quartier am Schnittpunkt der tradierten Stadtteile Westend und Bockenheim neu zu entwickeln und mit Leben zu füllen. Die damalige Oberbürgermeisterin Petra Roth erarbeitete hierfür ein visionäres Konzept: Der »Kulturcampus Bockenheim« sollte renommierte Kultureinrichtungen wie die Hochschule für Musik und Darstellende Kunst, das Ensemble Modern und die Forsythe Company in einem klimaneutralen Modellquartier mit bezahlbarem Wohnraum verbinden. Obgleich die kommunale Wohnungsbaugesellschaft *ABG Frankfurt Holding* schon 2011 einen ersten Schritt unternahm und das Areal vom Land Hessen erwarb, ist die Verwirklichung des Kulturcampus noch immer offen.

Realisiert wurde im Auftrag der ABG bislang nur die ursprünglich als Auftakt gedachte Blockrandbebauung an der nördlichen Spitze des ehemaligen Campus Bockenheim, deren drei übereck geführte Wohnhäuser von unterschiedlichen Architekturbüros geplant wurden. *Stefan Forster Architekten* entwickelte hierfür ein Eckhaus mit 58 Mietwohnungen und einer Einzelhandelsfläche in prominenter Lage am Carlo-Schmid-Platz, dessen großzügig bemessene Loggien und Fensterfronten auf die historischen Bauten seiner Umgebung blicken. Neben dem benachbarten Bockenheimer Depot – ein ehemaliger Straßenbahn-Betriebshof, der heute als Spielstätte der Städtischen Bühnen genutzt wird – prägt vor allem die Bockenheimer Warte als zentraler Platz mit dem gleichnamigen mittelalterlichen Wehrturm das Umfeld.

Zum Platz hin öffnet sich das Gebäude mit geschwungenen Balkonen, die das Motiv der abgerundeten Ecke aufnehmen und Assoziationen an die Architektur der »Weißen Stadt« in Tel Aviv hervorrufen. Ein Spiel aus Licht und Schatten bestimmt die Fassadengestaltung, deren ausgeprägte plastische Gliederung, Gesimsbänder und Verputzsprünge die Qualitäten gründerzeitlicher Stadthäuser neu interpretieren. Der dunkle Klinkersockel nimmt Bezüge zur Materialität des Bockenheimer Depots auf und hält durch die abweichende Farbigkeit zugleich Distanz. Das im Passivhausstandard errichtete Wohnhaus bietet eine Mischung aus geförderten Miet- und frei finanzierten Eigentumswohnungen und leistet somit einen Beitrag zur sozialen Durchmischung des Quartiers.

Founded in 1914, Bockenheim Campus was the main site of Frankfurt's Goethe University for almost 100 years. With the move of the social and natural sciences faculties to Westend and Riedberg, the old campus will gradually be given over to new functions by 2022. In the early 2000s this was identified as an opportunity to develop a new district at the interface between the traditional districts of Westend and Bockenheim, and to fill it with life. The mayor at the time, Petra Roth, produced a visionary concept for this: the "Bockenheim Cultural Campus", bringing together renowned cultural institutions such as the Frankfurt University of Music and Performing Arts, the Ensemble Modern and the Forsythe Company in a climate-neutral model district with affordable housing. Although in 2011 the local-authority housing company *ABG Frankfurt Holding* took the first step in this project by buying the site from the State of Hessen, it is at present unclear whether the "Cultural Campus" will go ahead.

So far the only new construction has been on the northern tip of the former Bockenheim Campus. Commissioned by ABG, this had been intended as the start of the project. The three corner apartment buildings in this residential block were planned by different architectural practices. *Stefan Forster Architekten* developed a corner building in a prominent location on Carlo-Schmid-Platz with 58 rental apartments and a retail unit. The generous loggias and window fronts on this new building look out on the historic buildings in the immediate environment. Alongside the neighbouring Bockenheim Depot (a former tram depot now used as a venue by the city's theatres), another very distinctive feature is the Bockenheim Warte, a mediaeval tower and a station of the same name, that occupy a central position.

Towards the square the building opens up with curved balconies that take up the motif of the rounded corner, awakening associations with the architecture of Tel Aviv's "White City". An interplay of light and shade characterises the façade design, its distinct sculptural articulation, continuous cornices and rendered moulding re-interpreting the qualities of late 19th-century urban buildings. The dark clinker-brick base storey references the materiality of Bockenheimer Depot while also, through its differing colouration, maintaining a distance. Constructed to the passive house standard, this residential building offers a mix of subsidised rental apartments and privately financed freehold flats. As such it makes a contribution to social mixing in the district.

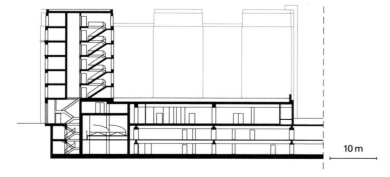

Querschnitt Wohnhaus mit Supermarkt und Tiefgarage • Cross section of residential building with supermarket and underground parking

Programm • Scope: 58 Wohnungen, Supermarkt • 58 apartments, supermarket
Geschossfläche (BGF) • Floor area (gross): 7120 m²
Fertigstellung • Completion: 2015
Bauherr • Client: ABG Frankfurt Holding
Mitarbeit • Project team: Moritz Kaiser, Jelena Duchrow, Zoltan Lepenye, Cristina Naranjo, Wiebke Nolte, Manuel Rhöse, Julia Tamm
Adresse • Address: Gabriel-Riesser-Weg 12–14, Gräfstraße 94, 60487 Frankfurt am Main

← Blick über die Bockenheimer Warte und den Carlo-Schmid-Platz mit Wehrturm (vorne rechts), Bockenheimer Depot (dahinter) und Europaturm (hinten links)
View over the Bockenheimer Warte and Carlo-Schmid-Platz with mediaeval tower (front right), Bockenheim Depot (behind it) and Europaturm (back left)
→ Blick von Südwesten auf die Ecke Gräfstraße / Gabriel-Riesser-Weg • View from the southwest, junction of Gräfstraße / Gabriel-Riesser-Weg

Haus in der Stadt • City Building

Südseite des Gebäudes am Gabriel-Riesser-Weg • South side of the building on Gabriel-Riesser-Weg

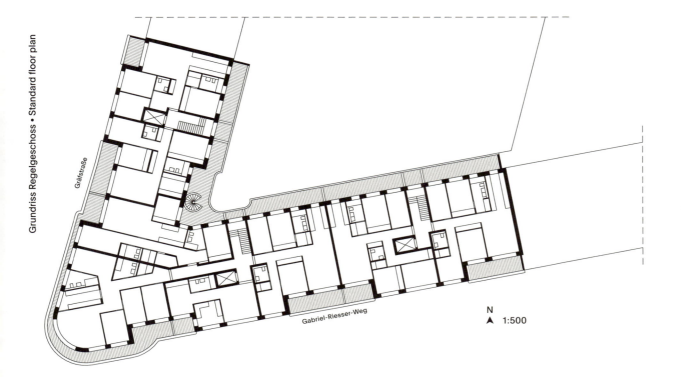

Grundriss Regelgeschoss • Standard floor plan

← Blick entlang der Gräfstraße nach Süden auf die Bockenheimer Warte und den Messeturm (im Hintergrund)
View along Gräfstraße towards the south of Bockenheim Warte and the Messeturm (in the background)

Nordseite des Gebäudes mit Hof • North side of the building with courtyard

145 Haus in der Stadt • City Building

Fassadendetails im Eingangsbereich am Gabriel-Riesser-Weg • Façade details in the entrance area on Gabriel-Riesser-Weg

2018   Schloßstraße
        Frankfurt am Main

Ruhig und versteckt liegt der Von-Bernus-Park im westlichen Teil von Frankfurt-Bockenheim. 1771 als Residenzpark im Stil eines englischen Landschaftsgartens angelegt, beherbergte er ursprünglich das im Zweiten Weltkrieg zerstörte Barockschloss von Prinzessin Henriette Amalie von Anhalt-Dessau. In der Nachkriegszeit schien der Bernuspark hingegen in Vergessenheit geraten: Die Eingänge waren kaum erkennbar, die Randbebauung unregelmäßig und ohne Gestalt. Seit den 1970er-Jahren befand sich neben dem Haupteingang an der Schloßstraße – deren Name noch an das Barockschloss erinnert – ein unscheinbarer, von wechselnden Lokalen genutzter Flachbau, der Anfang der 2010er-Jahre an die Projektentwickler Ardi Goldman und Ronny Weiner verkauft wurde. Während der Planungsphase für einen Ersatzneubau sanierte die Stadt Frankfurt auch den Bernuspark und wertete die Eingänge deutlich auf.

Für das Wohnhaus mit Kinderladen entwickelten *Stefan Forster Architekten* einen reduzierten, archaisch anmutenden Baukörper. In der Flucht der Schloßstraße bildet er den Kopf einer Häuserzeile aus den 1960er-Jahren. Trotz seiner zeitgenössischen Gestaltung erscheint der Neubau hier nicht dissonant: Prägende Elemente des Kontextes wie die Bebauungskante, die Kubatur und die Figur des traufständigen Satteldachs werden (mit Ausnahme einer quer zur Straße stehenden Hochhausscheibe) aufgenommen und neu interpretiert. Der zeichenhafte, auf die primäre Wirkung von Material, Proportion und Farbe vertrauende Bau erzeugt eine klar Raumkante zum Park hin und macht dessen Eingang wieder sichtbar. Die Signalwirkung wird durch die allseitige Verwendung von rot geflammten Wasserstrichklinkern mit durchgefärbten Fugen noch verstärkt. Von den Beton-Fensterbänken über die Textilscreens bis hin zu den Brüstungen aus Streckmetall sind sämtliche Fassadenelemente in korrespondierenden Rottönen gehalten. Als einzige Ausnahme wurde aus Kostengründen die rückwärtige Fluchttreppe in verzinktem Stahl ausgeführt. Tiefe Fensterlaibungen und in das Volumen eingeschnittene Loggien spinnen das typologische Thema der »Urhütte« weiter.

Die Straßen- und Giebelseiten sind mit einem schlichten vier- bzw. fünfachsigen Fensterraster strukturiert. Nach Süden öffnen sich großzügige Loggien mit bodentiefen Fenstern sowie der Kita-Garten zum Park hin. Lediglich die aus der Achse verschobenen Eingänge und die zum Hochhaus vermittelnde Erdgeschosswand brechen die strenge Symmetrie auf. Das Wohnhaus Schloßstraße bietet Raum für einen Kinderladen, mit Geschäftsräumen im ersten Obergeschoss, und 13 Mietwohnungen.

Von-Bernus-Park is a quiet, almost hidden spot in the western part of the district of Bockenheim in Frankfurt. Created in 1771 in the English landscape style, this was originally a residence park around the Baroque palace of Princess Henriette Amalie von Anhalt-Dessau. The palace was destroyed in the Second World War and in the post-war period the park seemed to have been forgotten. Its entrances were hardly recognisable, the development around its perimeter was irregular and without form. From the 1970s onwards, next to the main entrance on Schloßstraße (which means castle street), there was an unremarkable flat-roofed building, occupied by various cafés and bars over the years. This building was sold shortly after 2010 to project developers Ardi Goldman and Ronny Weiner. During the planning phase for a replacement building, the City of Frankfurt also regenerated Von-Bernus-Park and significantly upgraded the entrances.

For the new apartment block with children's day nursery, *Stefan Forster Architekten* developed a reduced, archaic-looking building volume. Along the line of Schloßstraße it stands at the end of a sequence of 1960s residential blocks. Despite its contemporary design, the new building does not jar in this context, as it takes up and re-interprets distinctive elements from its surroundings, e.g. the line of development, the cubic volume, the figure of the pitched roof with the ridge parallel to the street (with the exception of a high-rise block standing at a right angle to the street). The symbolic structure, deriving its impression from the primary effect of materials, proportion and colour, sets up a clear spatial line to Von-Bernus-Park, making the entrance to the park once again easy to see. Its strong presence is further enhanced through the use of red-flamed water-struck clinker bricks with mortar coloured to match. From the concrete window sills to the textile screens and the parapets of expanded metal – all elements in the façade are kept to the same tone of red. The only exception, for reasons of cost, is the emergency staircase at the back which is made of galvanised steel. Deep window reveals and loggias carved out of the building volume continue the typological theme of the "primitive hut".

The street faces and the gable ends are articulated by windows spaced on a simple grid of four or five axes. Spacious loggias with floor-to-ceiling windows open towards the park on the south side, as does the garden of the children's nursery. The strict symmetry is broken only by the entrances, positioned off-centre, and the wall of the ground floor which continues to the high-rise. This new building on Schloßstraße provides space for a children´s day nursery, offices on the first floor and 13 rental apartments above.

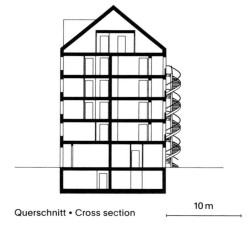

Querschnitt • Cross section   10 m

Programm • Scope: 13 Wohnungen, Kinderladen • 13 apartments, children's day nursery
Geschossfläche (BGF) • Floor area (gross): 1600 m²
Fertigstellung • Completion: 2018
Bauherr • Client: Goldman / Weiner GbR
Mitarbeit • Project team: Sonja Wollersheim, Frank Baum, Ildikó Návay
Adresse • Address: Schloßstraße 24, 60486 Frankfurt am Main

← Blick nach Westen entlang der Schloßstraße und des Von-Bernus-Parks • View towards the west along Schloßstraße and of Von-Bernus-Park
→ Blick von Norden auf das Wohnhaus an der Schloßstraße • View from the north of the apartment block on Schloßstraße

Fassadenansicht mit Verbindung zum Nachbargebäude · Façade elevation with connection to neighbouring building

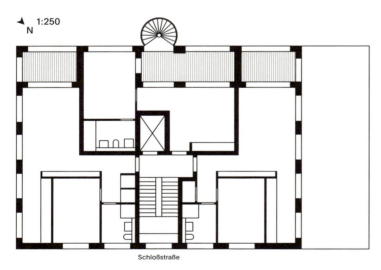

Grundriss Regelgeschoss · Standard floor plan

Schloßstraße

← Fassadenansicht der Parkseite mit Fluchttreppe • Facade elevation of the park side with emergency staircase
↓ Blick über den Spielplatz des Kinderladens auf die Parkseite des Gebäudes • View across the playground of the children's day nursery on the park side of the building

Schloßstraße

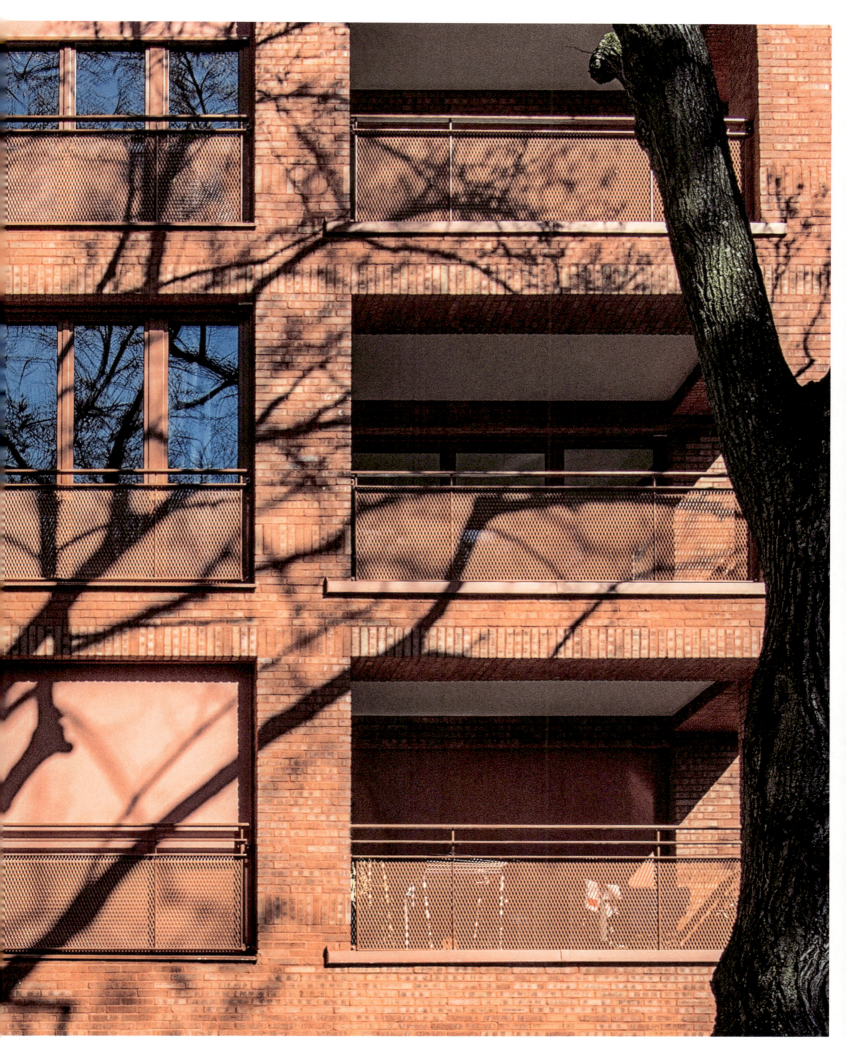

Fassadendetails von Süden • Façade details from the south

2017 Sandweg
Frankfurt am Main

Seit 1948 befand sich an der Ecke von Sandweg und Wingertstraße nicht nur eine der ältesten inhabergeführten, sondern auch eine der letzten kleinen Tankstellen inmitten eines Frankfurter Stadtviertels. Anfang 2011 verkaufte der langjährige Betreiber das 1.800 Quadratmeter große Gelände an den Projektentwickler *GeRo Real Estate*. An der Schnittstelle der beiden Stadtteile Bornheim und Ostend, in einem gewachsenen Wohnquartier unweit des Frankfurter Zoos und der Berger Straße, entstanden in der Folge 31 Eigentumswohnungen in einem Eckhaus mit Ladeneinheit und einem Doppelhaus im Innenhof. Wie später beim Campus Bockenheim lässt auch das Haus am Sandweg Bezüge zur Architektur der »Weißen Stadt« in Tel Aviv erkennen. Mit den Balkonen, die sich zu beiden Seiten über beinahe die gesamte Länge des Hauses spannen, und den tief eingeschnittenen Dachterrassen evoziert es Bilder, die an mediterrane Häuser oder ein Schiff an einer Strandpromenade denken lassen.

Bei aller Zitierfreude erscheint der Neubau jedoch nicht fremd. Proportionen und Maßstab des Hauses folgen der umliegenden Bebauung und wurden, unter Berücksichtigung der Baufluchten, lediglich neu interpretiert. Wo die Straßenfronten entlang des Sandwegs den Blockrand präzise weiterführen, wird dieser an der Wingertstraße leicht eingerückt. In dem so gewonnenen Abstand zwischen Straße und Haus sind Privatgärten angelegt, die mit einer Klinkermauer und einer dahinterliegenden Hecke – eine für Gründerzeitquartiere typische Vorgartensituation – eingefasst wurden. Details wie der profilierte Klinkersockel, die viertelkreisförmig abgerundeten Balustraden der Loggien und die überhöhten Ecken lassen den Baukörper im Stadtraum leicht und elegant erscheinen. Entstanden sind so flexibel geschnittene und hochwertig ausgestattete Ein- bis Vierzimmerwohnungen mit Privatgärten im Erdgeschoss sowie Balkonen und Loggien bzw. Dachterrassen in den Obergeschossen. Im Innenhof nimmt ein Doppelhaus mit Patio die Dimensionen der früheren Kfz-Werkstatt auf.

From 1948 onwards, one of Frankfurt's oldest independent petrol stations and one of the last such small operators in the inner city, stood at the corner of Sandweg and Wingertstraße. In early 2011 the long-term owner sold the 1,800 square-metre site to the project developer *GeRo Real Estate*. Subsequently 31 freehold apartments were built here at the interface of the two urban districts of Bornheim and Ostend, in an established residential district not far from Frankfurt Zoo and Berger Straße. The new development consists of a corner block with shop unit, along with a pair of semi-detached houses in the interior courtyard. As later with the Bockenheim Campus project, this building on Sandweg displays clear references to the architecture of Tel Aviv's "White City". The balconies that run almost the entire length of the building on both sides, and the deeply indented roof terraces, evoke images of Mediterranean houses or a cruise ship moored at a quayside.

Despite these references, the new building does not seem alien. The proportions and scale of the building echo that of the surrounding development, and were simply re-interpreted, taking into account the line of development along the street. While the street front along Sandweg traces the block edge precisely, on Wingertstraße the front is set back slightly. Private gardens occupy the space thus created between the street and the building; they are bordered by a clinker-brick wall and a hedge – a typical front-garden situation in late 19th-century urban districts. Details such as the profiled clinker base storey, the quarter-circles of the balustrades of the loggias and the raised corner sections give the building volume a light, elegant impression. The one- to four-room apartments, with a high-spec finish, have flexible ground plans; on the ground floor they have private gardens, and on the upper storeys balconies, loggias or roof terraces. In the courtyard, a pair of semi-detached houses with patio occupy the space where the garage workshop used to be.

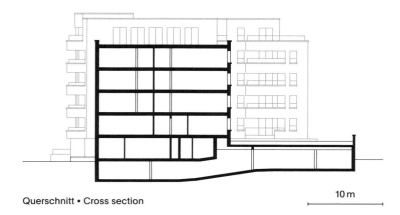

Querschnitt • Cross section — 10 m

Programm • Scope: 31 Wohnungen, Doppelhaus, Ladeneinheit • 31 apartments, two semi-detached houses, shop unit
Geschossfläche (BGF) • Floor area (gross): 4620 m²
Fertigstellung • Completion: 2013
Bauherr • Client: GeRo Sandweg-Projektentwicklungs GmbH & Co. KG
Mitarbeit • Project team: Nina Bölinger, Florian Kraft, Marco Leiser
Adresse • Address: Sandweg 82–84, Wingertstraße 5, 60316 Frankfurt am Main

Südseite des Gebäudes an der Ecke Sandweg / Wingertstraße • South side of the building, junction of Sandweg / Wingertstraße

Blick von Westen auf die Ecke Sandweg / Wingertstraße
View from the west, junction of Sandweg / Wingertstraße

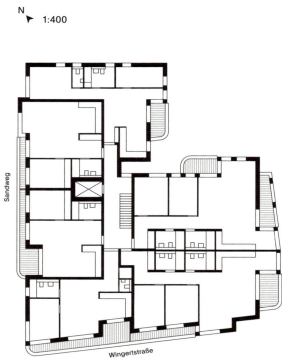

Grundriss Regelgeschoss (mit Dachaufsicht Doppelhaus) • Standard floor plan (with top view of the semi-detached houses)

Sandweg

Blick über den Hof nach Westen • View across the courtyard towards the west

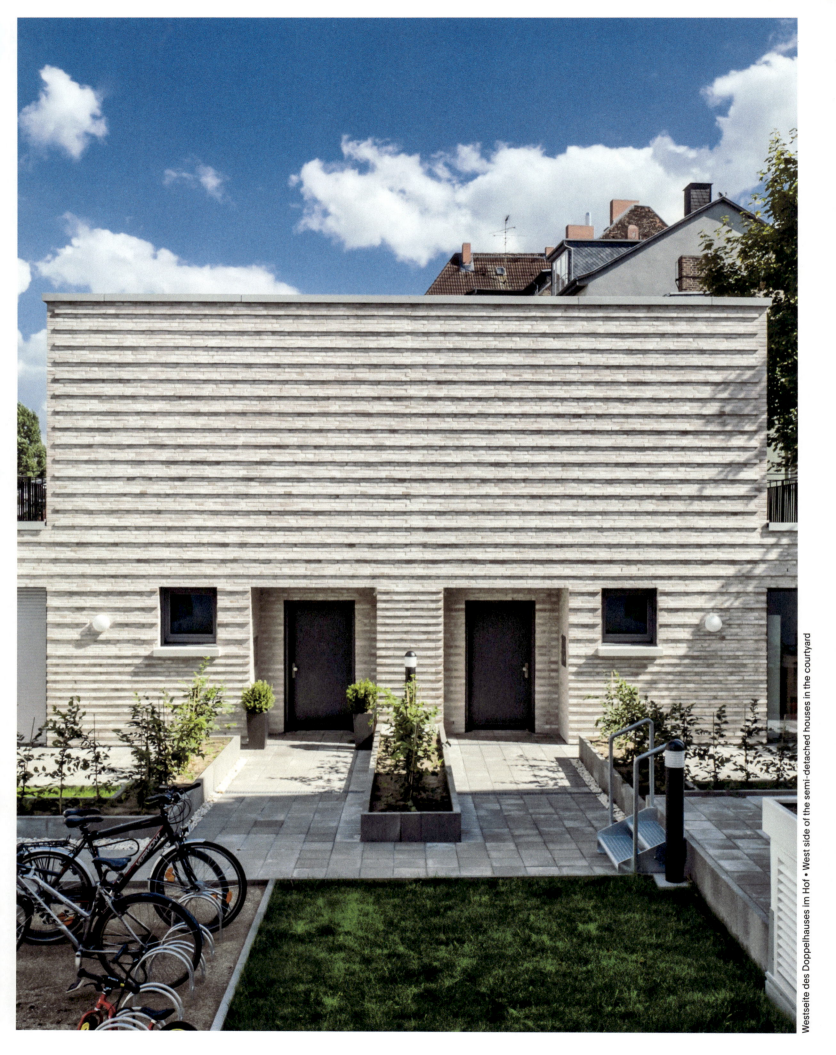

Westseite des Doppelhauses im Hof • West side of the semi-detached houses in the courtyard

2017 Wohnen auf Naxos
Living on Naxos
Frankfurt am Main

Die Geschichte von »Naxos« reicht bis in das 19. Jahrhundert zurück. Auf dem Areal zwischen Sandweg und Wittelsbacherallee im Frankfurter Ostend gründete die »Naxos Union« 1871 eine Fabrik zur Produktion von Schleifmaschinen. Mehr als hundert Jahre später war damit Schluss: Der Verkauf an die Rothenberger Gruppe führte im Zuge einer Produktionsverlagerung Ende der 1980er-Jahre zur Aufgabe des Werks. Nach jahrelangem Leerstand kaufte die Stadt Frankfurt 1999 erste Teile des Areals; 2006 folgte die denkmalgeschützte Haupthalle, die als sogenannte Naxoshalle als einziges Relikt des ehemaligen Industrieareals erhalten blieb und heute das freie Theater Willy Praml beherbergt. Die nördlich und östlich davon gelegenen Nebenhallen wurden schließlich 2008 zum Gegenstand eines Architektenwettbewerbs unter Federführung der kommunalen Wohnungsbaugesellschaft *ABG Frankfurt Holding*. Anstelle der Hallen sollten insgesamt knapp 180 Wohnungen entstehen – zu gut zwei Dritteln für die ABG im nördlichen sowie zu einem Drittel für eine Gruppe von sechs kleineren Genossenschaften im östlichen Teil.

Der Entwurf von *Stefan Forster Architekten* für das Areal nördlich der Naxoshalle sah einen lang gestreckten Riegelbau vor, der auf die örtlichen Gegebenheiten reagiert. Um den prägenden Baumbestand entlang der Wingertstraße erhalten zu können, wurde das Gebäude von der Straße eingerückt. Die so entstandene Vorgartenzone fungiert als Puffer zwischen Straße und Haus und nimmt Funktionen wie Fahrradstellplätze und Spielorte für Kinder auf. Die kammartige Struktur, die mit ihren sechs Quergebäuden den Längstrakt durchbricht, lockert die Ansicht zur Straße und ermöglicht eine optimale Belichtung. In den dazwischenliegenden Höfen sind die Privatgärten der Erdgeschosswohnungen angesiedelt. Die Rückseite der Anlage orientiert sich mit durchlaufenden Balkonen und Loggien zur denkmalgeschützten Naxoshalle und greift deren liegende Form auf.

Das Prinzip der in die Umgebung ausgreifenden Kämme bestimmt nicht nur den Grundriss, sondern auch die Höhenentwicklung: Mit sechs Geschossen überragen die Quergebäude den Längstrakt um ein Geschoss, was der gesamten Anlage einen eigenen Rhythmus verleiht und zugleich Raum für die Terrassen der Dachgeschosswohnungen bietet. Im Osten, an der Ecke von Wingertstraße und Wittelsbacherallee, wird der Blockrand durch ein siebengeschossiges Eckhaus konventionell geschlossen. Das wiederkehrende Element des durchlaufenden Klinkersockels betont dabei den Zusammenhang des Wohnkomplexes. Realisiert wurden je zur Hälfte Eigentums- und Mietwohnungen, die überwiegend beidseitig orientiert sind und je nach Lage über großzügige Gärten, Loggien oder Terrassen verfügen.

The story of "Naxos" goes back to the 19th century. In 1871, on the site between Sandweg and Wittelsbacheralle in Frankfurt's Ostend district, Naxos-Union built a factory to manufacture grinding machines. Over 100 years later the factory shut down after the company was sold to the Rothenberger Group and operations were moved to another site at the end of the 1980s. For years the site remained unused until 1999 when the City of Frankfurt purchased sections of it. In 2006 the City also bought the main factory building, which was a listed structure. This hall, called Naxoshalle, is the only remaining relic of the former industrial complex. Today it is the home of the Willy Praml theatre company. In 2008, the ancillary halls to the north and east then became the subject of an architectural competition organised by the local housing association, *ABG Frankfurt Holding*. The aim was to build around 180 apartments in place of the halls – two-thirds of them for ABG in the northern part, and one-third for a group of six smaller housing associations in the eastern part.

The design by *Stefan Forster Architekten* for the site to the north of Naxoshalle, envisaged a long, linear building that responds to the local context. In order to retain the characteristic trees along Wingertstraße, the building was set back from the street. The front-garden zone thus created operates as a buffer between the street and the building, providing space for facilities such as bicycle parking and areas for children to play. The indented line of the building, with six tracts piercing the linear structure at right angles, loosens up the street face and enables maximum exploitation of daylight. The courtyards between these tracts contain the private gardens of the ground-floor apartments. Oriented towards Naxoshalle, the rear of the complex features continuous balconies and loggias, echoing the horizontality of the hall.

The principle of a "comb-like" structure, or indented outline projecting into the surrounding space, underlies not only the plan of the building, but also its height development. At six floors in height, the crosswise sections rise above the linear tract by one storey, a device that gives a distinctive rhythm to the whole complex, while also creating space for the terraces of the roof-top apartments. In the east, at the junction of Wingertstraße and Wittelsbacherallee, the edge of the block is conventionally finished off with a seven-storey corner building. The recurring element of the continuous clinker base storey emphasises the coherence of the residential complex. Half of the apartments are rental, the other half freehold; most of them are dual-aspect and, depending on their exact position, they have a generous garden, a loggia or a terrace.

Längsschnitt • Longitudinal section 10 m

Wohnungen • Apartments: 116
Geschossfläche (BGF) • Floor area (gross): 15 000 m²
Fertigstellung • Completion: 2013
Bauherr • Client: ABG Frankfurt Holding
Mitarbeit • Project team: Eleanor Lucke, Benjamin Metz, Jelena Duchrow, Peter Gallo, Manuel Rhöse, Andreas Wenger, Cristina Naranjo
Adresse • Address: Wingertstraße 22–32, Wittelsbacherallee 35, 60316 Frankfurt am Main

Blick von Nordwesten auf das Haus Wingertstraße 22 • View from the northwest of the building at Wingertstraße 22

Vorgartenzone an der Wingertstraße von Norden • Front garden zone on Wingertstraße from the north

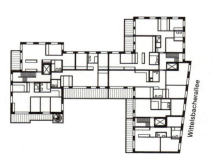

Grundriss Regelgeschoss • Standard floor plan

174 Wohnen auf Naxos • Living on Naxos

Blick entlang der Vorgartenzone nach Südosten • View along the front garden zone towards the southeast

Blick nach Nordwesten über die Privatgärten auf der Hofseite • View towards the northwest of the private gardens on the courtyard side

Wohnen auf Naxos • Living on Naxos

2016 Adickesallee
Frankfurt am Main

Vor Gründung der Bundesrepublik galt Frankfurt am Main für einen kurzen Moment als Favorit im Rennen um den zukünftigen Regierungssitz. Um Fakten zu schaffen, hatte Oberbürgermeister Walter Kolb bereits ein Regierungsviertel im Norden der Stadt ausweisen und einen Plenarsaal bauen lassen. Durch einen Coup des späteren Bundeskanzlers Adenauer stimmte der Parlamentarische Rat im Mai 1949 jedoch überraschend mit 33 zu 29 Stimmen für Bonn – die Hauptstadtträume Frankfurts waren geplatzt, der Plenarsaal wurde zum Funkhaus des Hessischen Rundfunks umgenutzt. Zur Kompensation erhielt Frankfurt in der Nachkriegszeit einige Bundesbehörden, darunter die 1952 zwischen Adickesallee und Funkhaus errichtete Bundesanstalt für Landwirtschaft und Ernährung – als Außenstelle des Landwirtschaftsministeriums auch »Kartoffelministerium« genannt. Nach dem Umzug der Behörde 2005 stand der Gebäudekomplex zehn Jahre leer und wurde schließlich durch das Appartementhaus Adickesallee und ein Wohnquartier ersetzt.

Kubatur und Dimension des Neubaus resultieren aus einer Analyse der städtebaulichen Situation. Entlang der stark befahrenen Adickesallee, die den nördlichen Abschnitt des Frankfurter Alleenrings bildet, fügt sich das Appartementhaus in eine Abfolge großformatiger Gebäude mit streng gerasterten Fassaden – von der Bundesbank und dem Uni-Campus Westend bis hin zum Polizeipräsidium und der Frankfurt School of Finance and Management. Nach Süden ist die Bebauungsstruktur kleinteiliger und eher gründerzeitlich geprägt; nach Norden schließen Siedlungen in offener Bauweise an. Der U-förmige, neungeschossige Baukörper übernimmt die Dimension der benachbarten Solitäre und bildet eine klare Raumkante zum Alleenring. Mit seinen rückwärtigen Seitenflügeln wird eine zukünftige Anschlussbebauung in Form eines städtischen Blocks ermöglicht. Die stark profilierte Fassade vertraut ganz auf die Wirkung von rötlichem Klinker und vermeidet bewusst Hinweise auf die Nutzung des Hauses. Turmartig überhöhte Ecken, die im Westen neun, im Osten acht Geschosse umfassen, reagieren auf die Nachbarbebauung und machen das Gebäude im Stadtraum identifizierbar. Zwei kräftige Gesimse gliedern die Fassade klassisch in Sockel, Schaft und »Kapitell« – hier repräsentiert durch ein zurückversetztes Staffelgeschoss. Die Strenge der Straßenfront wird auf der Rückseite durch alternierend angeordnete Balkone gelockert.

Before the founding of the Federal Republic of Germany, Frankfurt am Main was for a short time the favourite in the running to be nominated as the new seat of government. To give his city the best chance of securing that prize, Frankfurt's Lord Mayor, Walter Kolb, designated an area in the north of the city as a government district, and even built a plenary hall there. However, in a surprise move by Konrad Adenauer, who later became Federal Chancellor, the Parliamentary Council voted for Bonn instead, with 33 votes to 29. Frankfurt's dreams of being the capital were dashed, the plenary hall was re-functioned as the broadcasting house (Funkhaus) of Hessischer Rundfunk. As compensation, in the post-war years Frankfurt did receive a number of federal authorities, among them a part of the Ministry of Agriculture – the Federal Office for Agriculture and Food, for which a new building was constructed in 1952 between Adickesallee and the Funkhaus. After this authority moved out in 2005 the complex of buildings stood empty for ten years until finally being replaced by the Adickesallee Apartment House and a residential estate.

The cubic volume and the dimensions of the new building result from an analysis of the immediate urban environment. Along Adickesallee, a very busy road that forms the northern section of the city's Alleenring, the apartment block takes its place in a succession of large-scale buildings with strictly regular façades – from the Bundesbank and the Westend university campus to the police headquarters and the Frankfurt School of Finance and Management. Towards the south the structure of development is much smaller in scale and also features older buildings from the latter part of the 19th century; to the north are residential estates with a more open character. The U-shaped, up to nine-storey high building volume adopts the dimensions of the neighbouring solitaire and forms a clear spatial border to the Alleenring. With the right-angled wings at the ends, the building leaves scope for extension at a later date to complete the urban block. The strongly profiled façade derives its effect from the red clinker brick, and deliberately avoids reference to the function of the building. Tower-like corners – nine storeys high in the west, eight in the east – are a reaction to the neighbouring development and an immediately recognisable identifier in the urban landscape. Two strongly modelled cornices articulate the façade classically into a base section, a shaft and a "capital", represented here by a recessed top storey. The rigour of the street face is relaxed at the back by alternately aligned balconies.

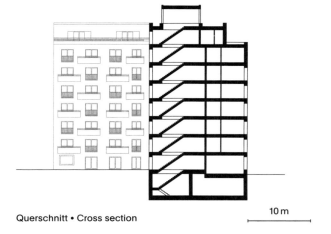

Querschnitt • Cross section — 10 m

Programm • Scope: 332 Wohnungen, Café • 332 apartments, café
Geschossfläche (BGF) • Floor area (gross): 14 500 m²
Fertigstellung • Completion: 2016
Bauherr • Client: RMW Wohnungsgesellschaft Frankfurt II GmbH
Mitarbeit • Project team: Holger Haas, Jelena Duchrow, Militsa Marinova, Peter Gallo, Neset Uguzoglu
Adresse • Address: Adickesallee 40, 60322 Frankfurt am Main

Blick von Südwesten auf die Ecke Bertramstraße / Adickesallee • View from the southwest, junction of Bertramstraße / Adickesallee

Südseite des Gebäudes an der Adickesallee • South side of the building on Adickesallee

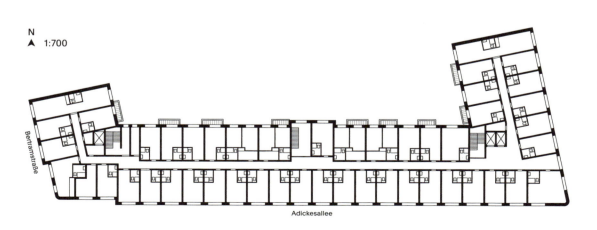

N 1:700

Bertramstraße

Adickesallee

Grundriss Regelgeschoss • Standard floor plan

182 Adickesallee

Fassadenansicht entlang der Adickesallee nach Westen • View of the façade along Adickesallee towards the west

Fassadendetails an der Adickesallee • Façade details on Adickesallee

Nordseite des Gebäudes an der Ostendstraße • North side of the building on Ostendstraße

Haus in der Stadt • City Building

Blick von Süden über den Hof • View from the south across the courtyard

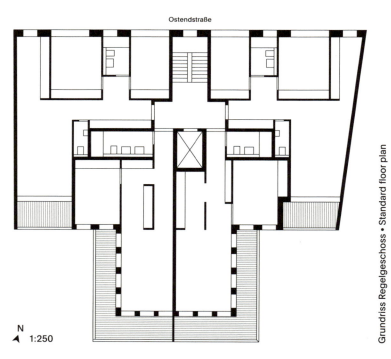

Grundriss Regelgeschoss • Standard floor plan

Ostendstraße

N 1:250

190 Ostendstraße

Fassadenansicht an der Ostendstraße • View of the façade, Ostendstraße

Haus in der Stadt • City Building

Eingangsbereich in der Ostendstraße • Entrance area on Ostendstraße

Blick entlang der Westseite des Gebäudes an der Windeckstraße (im Hintergrund die Europäische Zentralbank) • View along the west side of the building on Windeckstraße (in the background, the European Central Bank)

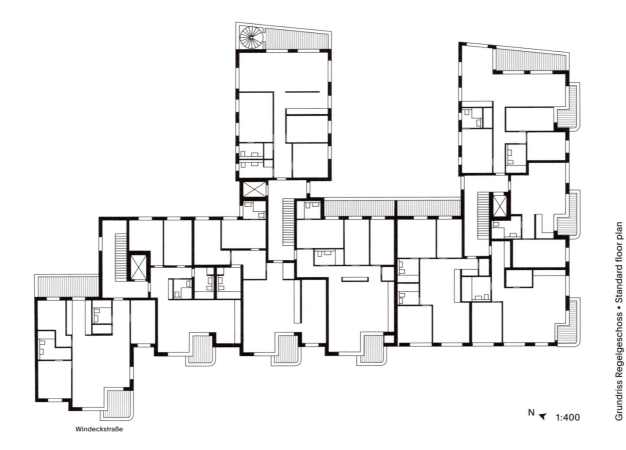

Grundriss Regelgeschoss • Standard floor plan 1:400

Westseite an der Windeckstraße • West side on Windeckstraße

198 Windeckstraße

Blick von Süden über die Vorgartenzone an der Windeckstraße • View from the south across the front garden zone on Windeckstraße

Fassadenansicht an der Windeckstraße • Facade elevation, Windeckstraße

2011 Wohn- und Geschäftshaus R7
R7 apartment and office block
Mannheim

»R7« ist der Name eines Straßenblocks in der gitterförmig aufgebauten Mannheimer Innenstadt, den sogenannten Quadraten. Dieses ursprünglich aus der Barockzeit stammende Straßenraster basiert als typische Planstadt auf einer Abfolge rechteckiger Blöcke und sich orthogonal kreuzender Straßen. Eine Ausnahme stellt die bogenförmige Straße an der westlichen Seite von R7 dar, die dem Verlauf der mittelalterlichen Stadtmauer folgt. Hier wünschte sich die lokale Baugenossenschaft *Spar und Bau* ein Wohnhaus in einer möglichst zurückhaltenden Architektur, das zugleich die eigene Geschäftsstelle beherbergen sollte. Der Entwurf für das Wohn- und Geschäftshaus sah zunächst zwei unterschiedlich dimensionierte und miteinander verschränkte Baukörper vor, die in ihrer Höhe auf den Kontext reagierten – nach Norden auf den niedrigeren Blockrand, nach Süden auf ein Wohnhochhaus aus den 1950er-Jahren. Die beiden gegenüber dem Blockrand eingerückten Volumen nehmen nun einerseits den bogenförmigen Verlauf der Straße auf und stellen zugleich eine Verbindung zum Hochhaus her, das wiederum leicht schräg zur Straße steht. So ergibt sich in der Ansicht von Süden – seit 2016 durch eine neu geschaffene Passage des Einkaufszentrums Q6/Q7 zusätzlich aufgewertet – eine reizvolle Tiefenstaffelung von scheibenförmig erscheinenden Baukörpern.

Besondere Sorgfalt wurde auf die Materialisierung des Gebäudes gelegt, dessen massive, zweischalige Fassade aus hellbeigen Klinkern im wilden Verband an drei Seiten die Gebäudehülle bildet. Die rustikale Anmutung der im Wasserstrichverfahren produzierten Klinkersteine im Verbund mit den hellgrauen, leicht zurückversetzten Fugen verstärkt die monolithische Wirkung des Baukörpers, der seine Lebendigkeit einzig der aufwändigen Profilierung und dem feinen Farbspiel der Steine verdankt. Durch den regelmäßigen Rücksprung zweier Klinkerlagen im Sockelbereich ergibt sich zudem der Eindruck von horizontalen »Kanneluren« – ein Prinzip, das in den Obergeschossen durch umlaufende Gesimse, die Grenadierschicht über den Fenstern und einen Rillenverband zur Betonung der Fensterbänder fortgeführt wird. Die im selben Stein ausgeführte Grundstücksmauer betont den Zusammenhang des Ensembles und markiert zugleich die Straßenflucht, während sich die Hofseite – im Kontrast zur geordneten Vorderseite – mit durchgehenden Balkonen zum Lameygarten, einer aus dem 19. Jahrhundert stammenden städtischen Parkanlage, öffnet.

"R7" is the name of one of the blocks (known as "Quadrate") in Mannheim's inner city, the layout for which dates back to the 17th century. Typical of a planned town, it has rectangular blocks criss-crossed by a grid of streets. One street that does not conform to this grid, is a curving street on the west side of block R7 which follows the line of the mediaeval town wall. Here the local building association *Spar und Bau* wanted to build a residential block, quiet and restrained in appearance, in which its own main offices would also be located. The design for this block of apartments and offices was in the first place for two differently dimensioned and interlinked building volumes reacting through their height to the context – on the north side to the lower development along the block edge, and on the south to a residential high-rise from the 1950s. The two volumes, angled against the edge of the block, take up the curve of the street and also set up a connection to the high-rise, which is itself also at a slight angle to the street. So, seen from the south (since 2016 the area has been upgraded again with the addition of a new shopping centre, the Q6/7 Quartier), an interesting staggered arrangement of slab-like building volumes is revealed.

Special attention was paid to the materials used on the building: The result is a stone-like double-skinned façade of light-beige clinker brick in a random bond. The rustic impression of the waterstruck clinker bricks with pale-grey slightly recessed mortar emphasises the monolithic effect of the building volume. Careful moulding detail and the subtle tones of the brick give a lively impression to the façade. At ground-floor level double rows of bricks were set back slightly from the rest at regular intervals to look like horizontal "fluting". This principle is continued in the upper storeys in the form of wrap-around cornices, a row of bricks on end above the windows and a band of brickwork with alternate lines of recessed bricks that emphasise the windows. The wall around the plot, also built in the same brick, underlines the coherence of the ensemble and also marks the line of the street, while the courtyard side – in contrast to the front – opens up with continuous balconies to Lameygarten, an urban park laid out in the 19th century.

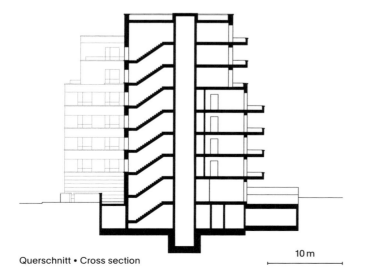

Querschnitt • Cross section   10 m

Programm • Scope: 34 Wohnungen, Geschäftsräume • 34 apartments, offices
Geschossfläche (BGF) • Floor area (gross): 4 800 m²
Fertigstellung • Completion: 2011
Bauherr • Client: Baugenossenschaft Spar- und Bauverein 1895 Mannheim eG
Mitarbeit • Project team: Martina Rüdiger, Jelena Duchrow, Wiebke Nolte, Andreas Wenger
Adresse • Address: R7, 3–6, 68161 Mannheim

Blick über die Straße nach Nordosten • View across the road towards the northeast

Fassadenansicht an der Westseite des Gebäudes • View of the façade, west side of the building

Grundriss Regelgeschoss • Standard floor plan

N 1:400

Ostseite des Gebäudekomplexes mit Vorgartenzone • East side of the building complex with front garden zone

Haus in der Stadt • City Building

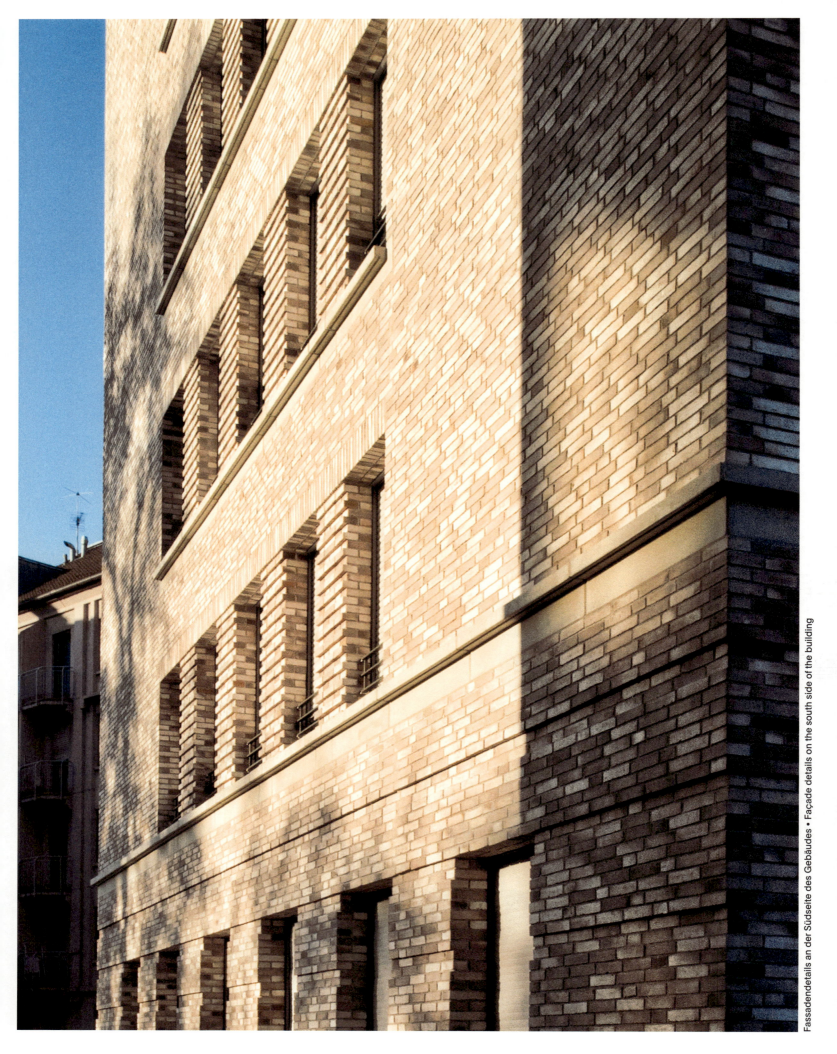

Fassadendetails an der Südseite des Gebäudes • Façade details on the south side of the building

2017 Unterrather Straße
      Düsseldorf

Die Wohnungsgenossenschaft Düsseldorf-Ost zählt zu den traditionsreichsten und größten Genossenschaften in Düsseldorf. Als sie sich 2012 zum Abbruch ihres aus den 1920er-Jahren stammenden Wohnhauses in der Unterrather Straße entschloss, hatte sie klare Ziele für einen Ersatzneubau vor Augen: Anstelle der einfachen, immer gleich geschnittenen Kleinstwohnungen sollten modern ausgestattete Ein- bis Fünfzimmerwohnungen mit Loggien und Terrassen für unterschiedliche Nutzergruppen entstehen. Der Abbruch des Altbaus, der mit seiner dunkelroten Klinkerfassade und der bewegten Dachlandschaft längst Teil der lokalen Identität geworden war, galt im Quartier zunächst als durchaus umstritten. Im gewachsenen Stadtteil Unterrath, im Norden von Düsseldorf gelegen, sollte der Neubau deshalb nicht nur städtebaulich sensibel integriert werden, sondern auch die spezifischen Qualitäten des Altbaus aufnehmen und fortschreiben.

Der nach einem gewonnenen Gutachterverfahren realisierte Entwurf orientiert sich in Form und Materialität am Vorgängergebäude und fügt sich wie ein Puzzlestück in die städtebauliche Situation ein: Die architektonische Gestalt des geschwungenen Riegelbaus wurde beibehalten und nach Süden um zwei rückwärtige Flügel ergänzt. Entlang der Unterrather Straße begleitet er den Straßenraum, der sich nach Westen aufweitet und mit dem Klinkeplatz einen kleinen Quartiersplatz bildet, von dem sich auch die alternative Bezeichnung »Klinkebogen« für das Wohnhaus ableitet. Die lang gestreckte, konvexe Biegung des Mittelteils spannt sich zwischen den niedrigeren Kopfseiten auf, die sich an der Höhe der Nachbarhäuser orientieren und mit Treppengiebeln verziert den Übergang von der städtisch-dichten Unterrather Straße in die beinahe dörflich geprägten Seitenstraßen akzentuieren.

Neben den unterschiedlichen Höhen entsteht die Dynamik der Fassade durch den Wechsel von auskragenden und eingeschnittenen Bauteilen wie Erkern und Loggien. Fortgesetzt wird die skulpturale Qualität des Baukörpers in Details wie den versetzten Klinkerlagen, der Grenadierschicht über den Fenstern und den durchlaufenden Gesimsen. Als Reminiszenz an die weiße Rückseite des Vorgängerbaus wurden die nach Süden anschließenden Seitenflügel hell verputzt und über einen schmalen Klinkersockel mit dem Haupthaus verbunden. Durch die U-förmige Anordnung des Ensembles entsteht ein geschützter und großzügig begrünter Innenhof.

The Wohnungsgenossenschaft Düsseldorf-Ost is one of the largest and longest-standing cooperative housing associations in Düsseldorf. When in 2012 it decided to demolish one of its 1920s apartment blocks, on Unterrather Straße, it had clear goals: The simple, small apartments from those early years, with their identical layouts, would give way to a new block, with modern one- to five-room apartments with loggias and terraces for different groups of occupants. Residents in the area, however, at first resisted the plan to demolish this old building, with its dark-red clinker brick façade and lively roof landscape, as it had become so much a part of the identity of the district. As a result, it was important for the new building in this established district of Unterrath, in the north of Düsseldorf, to not only sensitively integrate into its urban setting, but also reflect and continue the specific qualities of the 1920s building.

The chosen design, by *Stefan Forster Architekten*, emerged from an expert opinion procedure. In form and use of materials, it is oriented towards the previous building on this site and fits into the local urban situation like a piece of a jigsaw: The architectural design of the curved linear block was retained and extended towards the south by two wings at the rear. Along Unterrather Straße it follows the curving line of the street, which opens out towards the west to join Klinkeplatz in a small square, a situation which gives rise to the local nickname for the new building: "Klinkebogen" (clinker bend). The long convex curve of the middle section stretches between the lower-height end sections which, oriented towards the height of the neighbouring buildings and decorated with corbie or step gables, accentuate the transition from the denser urban development on Unterrather Straße to the almost village character of the side streets.

The dynamism in the façade originates not only from the different height development, but also from the alternation of cantilevered and inset components such as oriel windows and loggias. The sculptural quality of the building volume is continued in details such as the recessed layers of brick, the upright rows of bricks above the windows and the continuous cornices. As a reminder of the white rear façade of the previous building, the wing extending towards the south is rendered and painted in a light colour, and connected to the main building via a narrow clinker-brick base. The U-shape arrangement of the ensemble gives rise to space for a protected and landscaped inner courtyard.

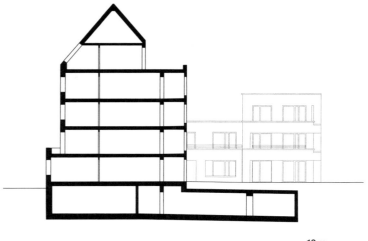

Querschnitt mit Seitenflügel • Cross section with side wing 10 m

Wohnungen • Apartments: 62
Geschossfläche (BGF) • Floor area (gross): 7 270 m²
Fertigstellung • Completion: 2017
Bauherr • Client: Wohnungsgenossenschaft Düsseldorf-Ost eG
Mitarbeit • Project team: Ute Streit, Jelena Duchrow, Frank Baum, Janos Lalik, Sandra Söhnel
Adresse • Address: Unterrather Straße 27–41, 40648 Düsseldorf

← Blick von Süden über den Klinkeplatz und die Unterrather Straße • View from the south across Klinkeplatz and Unterrather Straße
→ Westseite an der Unterrather Straße • West side on Unterrather Straße

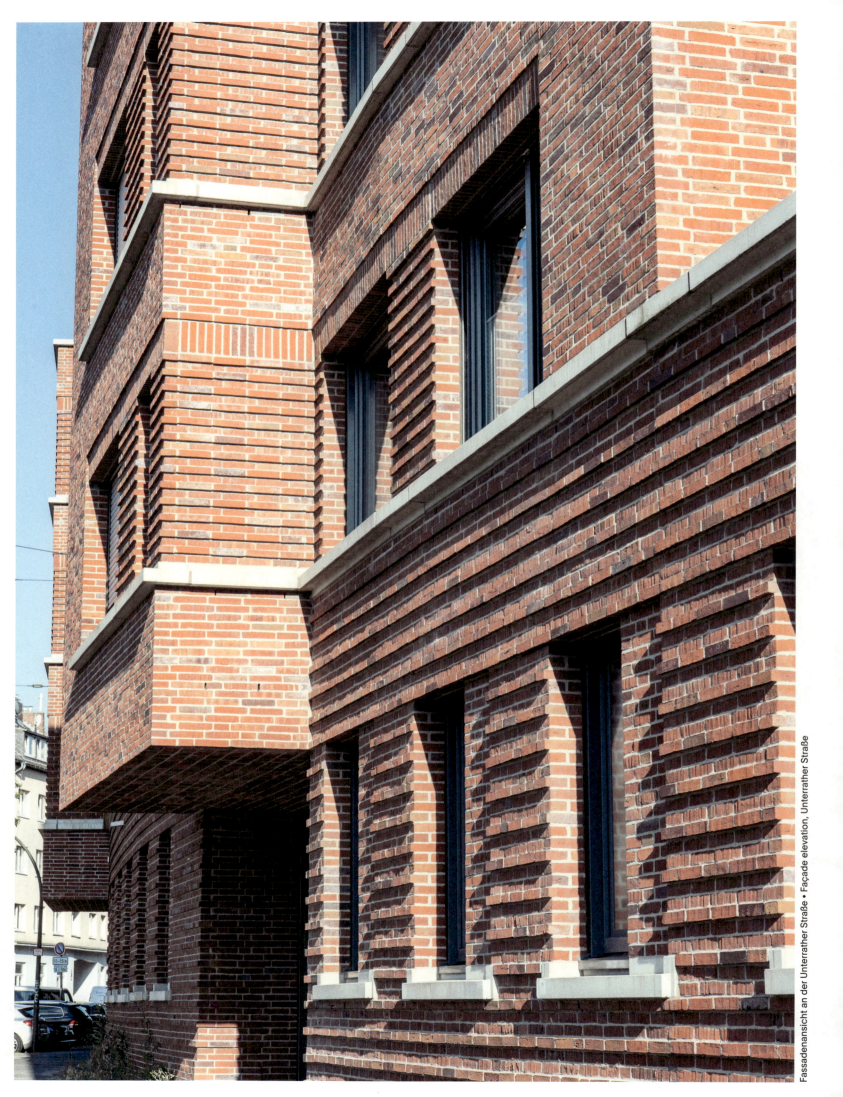

Fassadenansicht an der Unterrather Straße • Façade elevation, Unterrather Straße

2016   Französische Allee
       Hanau

Mit knapp 100.000 Einwohnern zählt Hanau zu den bedeutenden Mittelstädten im Rhein-Main-Gebiet. Die nach dem Zweiten Weltkrieg schmucklos wieder aufgebaute Innenstadt steht jedoch wegen ihrer Monotonie seit Jahren in der Kritik. Aufgrund der starken Kriegszerstörungen weist das als »Hanauer Neustadt« gegen Ende des 16. Jahrhunderts gegründete heutige Zentrum nur wenige historische Konstanten auf. Zu ihnen zählen etwa das schachbrettartige Straßenraster – Relikt der barocken Planstadt – und das Baudenkmal der Wallonisch-Niederländischen Kirche (1611), die bereits im Namen an die damalige starke Zuwanderung von calvinistischen Glaubensflüchtlingen aus Frankreich und den Spanischen Niederlanden erinnert. Nach der Zerstörung im Zweiten Weltkrieg wurde der kleinere, ehemals niederländische Teil der Doppelkirche wieder aufgebaut; der größere, aus einem Zwölfeck gebildete ehemals wallonische Teil blieb lediglich als Ruine erhalten. Seit der Aufstellung des städtebaulichen Rahmenplans »Südliche Innenstadt« 2010 befindet sich das Quartier um die Wallonisch-Niederländische Kirche, die von der Französischen Allee als einer Art Ringstraße umgeben wird, in einer Phase der Erneuerung.

Für die kommunale Wohnungsbaugesellschaft planten *Stefan Forster Architekten* den Ersatzneubau an der Ostseite des Platzes. Der 1952 errichtete Vorgängerbau wies gravierende Mängel der Bausubstanz auf und entsprach mit seinen zu kleinen Grundrissen, den engen Treppenhäusern und maroden Sanitäranlagen nicht mehr den zeitgemäßen Wohnstandards. Wie sein Vorgänger folgt der U-förmige, zurückhaltend gestaltete Neubau präzise dem Blockrand und bildet eine eindeutige Platzkante nach Westen aus. Die Proportionen des Baukörpers, die Materialität der Fassade und die Dachform orientieren sich am Leitfaden für die Gestaltung der Innenstadt, der sogenannten »Fassadenfibel«, und fügen sich in den Kontext der südlichen Innenstadt ein. Auf dem massiven Klinkersockel mit erhöhtem Erdgeschoss setzen drei Obergeschosse mit großen Verglasungen und unterschiedlichen Putzstrukturen an. Das rötliche Satteldach mit markanten Dachgauben ist an das historische Hanauer Stadtbild angelehnt. Die Wohnungen verfügen straßenseitig über eine Loggia und hofseitig über einen Balkon, die Dachgeschosswohnungen zu beiden Seiten über Terrassen. Im Zuge der Neuplanung wird nicht nur die Randbebauung an den drei Platzseiten – dem Süd-, West- und Ostcarré – erneuert, sondern auch der bisher als Parkplatz genutzte Kirchplatz wieder zu einem autofreien, parkartig gestalteten Stadtplatz umgewandelt.

With around 100,000 inhabitants, Hanau is a small but important city in the Rhine-Main area. Its urban centre, rebuilt after the Second World War, has however been criticised for years for being monotonous and without charm. What is the central area of Hanau today was founded in the late 16th century as a new town, but few historical constants survived the severe war damage. Among these are the chess-like street grid, a relic of the Baroque planned town, and the Walloon-Dutch Church (1611), whose name testifies to the influx of Calvinists from France and the Spanish Netherlands fleeing persecution for their beliefs. After 1945 the smaller, formerly Dutch part of this double church was rebuilt; the larger, formerly Walloon part, which had twelve sides, is preserved only as a ruin. In 2010 a master plan for urban development in the southern part of the town centre was drawn up and since then the area immediately around the Walloon-Dutch Church, bounded ring-road-like by Französische Allee, has been in a phase of regeneration.

The local authority housing association commissioned *Stefan Forster Architekten* to build a new residential block just to the east of the church. This was to replace a 1952 apartment building which had serious structural defects and no longer conformed to modern standards because the individual apartments were too small, the staircases were too narrow and the sanitary installations were dilapidated. Like its predecessor the unassuming U-shaped new block follows the outline of the city block precisely, and draws a clear borderline towards the west along the edge of the square. The proportions of the building volume, the materiality of the façade and the roof form adhere to the guidelines (the "façade bible") laid down for city-centre development, and blend into the context of the southern part of this central urban area. Rising above the clinker base with raised ground floor are three upper storeys with extensive glazing and a range of render detail. The reddish pitched roof with distinctive dormer windows is aligned with the historic building characteristics of Hanau. Each of the apartments has a loggia on the street side and a balcony on the courtyard side. The apartments on the top floor have roof terraces, overlooking the street and the inner courtyard. As part of the redevelopment of the area around the church, not only the buildings around the edge of the church square are being rebuilt (the blocks on the south, west and east sides), the church square itself, previously used as a car park, is being transformed back into a car-free, park-like urban green space.

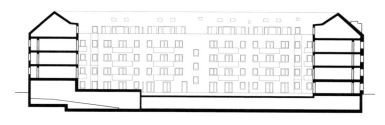

Querschnitt • Cross section 10 m

Wohnungen • Apartments: 57
Geschossfläche (BGF) • Floor area (gross): 5 820 m²
Fertigstellung • Completion: 2016
Bauherr • Client: Baugesellschaft Hanau GmbH
Mitarbeit • Project team: Nina Bölinger, Ulrich Ricker, Isabelle Heinsohn
Adresse • Address: Französische Allee 2–6, 63450 Hanau

← Blick über die Französische Allee nach Südosten • View across Französische Allee towards the southeast
→ Westseite des Gebäudes an der Ecke Französische Allee / Schützenstraße • West side of the building at the junction of Französische Allee / Schützenstraße

Haus in der Stadt • City Building

Fassadenansicht an der Französischen Allee • Façade elevation, Französische Allee

Siedlung
Housing Estate

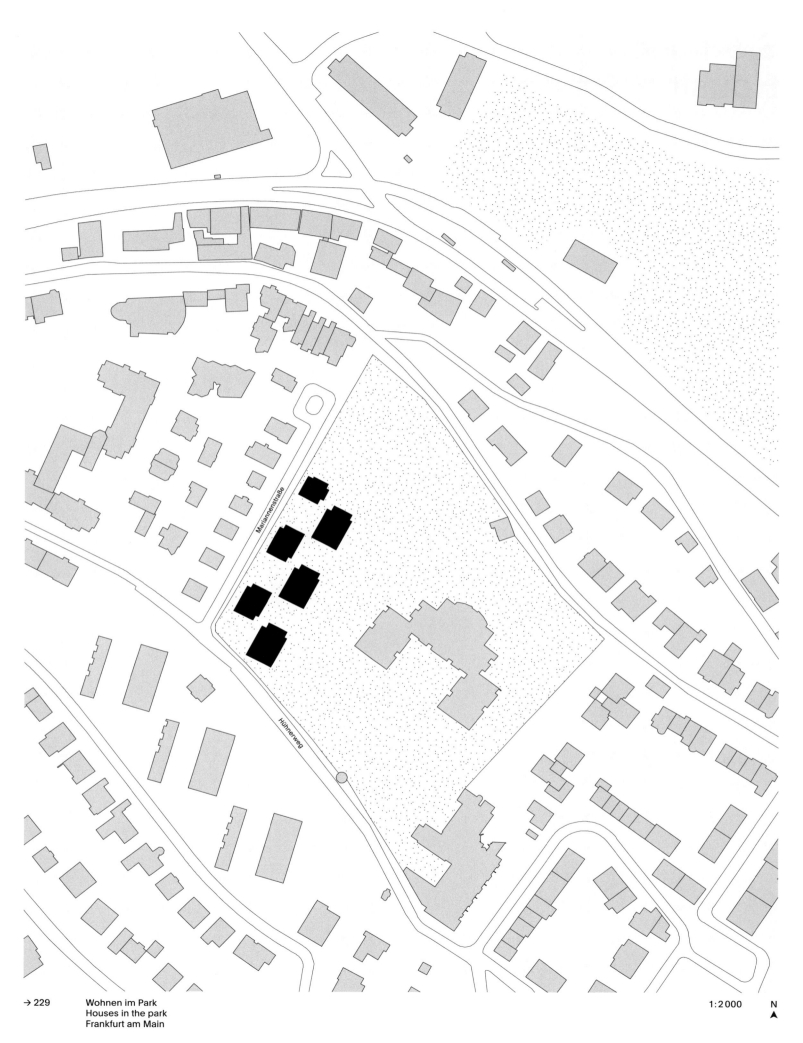

→ 229 Wohnen im Park
Houses in the park
Frankfurt am Main

226 Lagepläne • Site plans

1:2 000 N

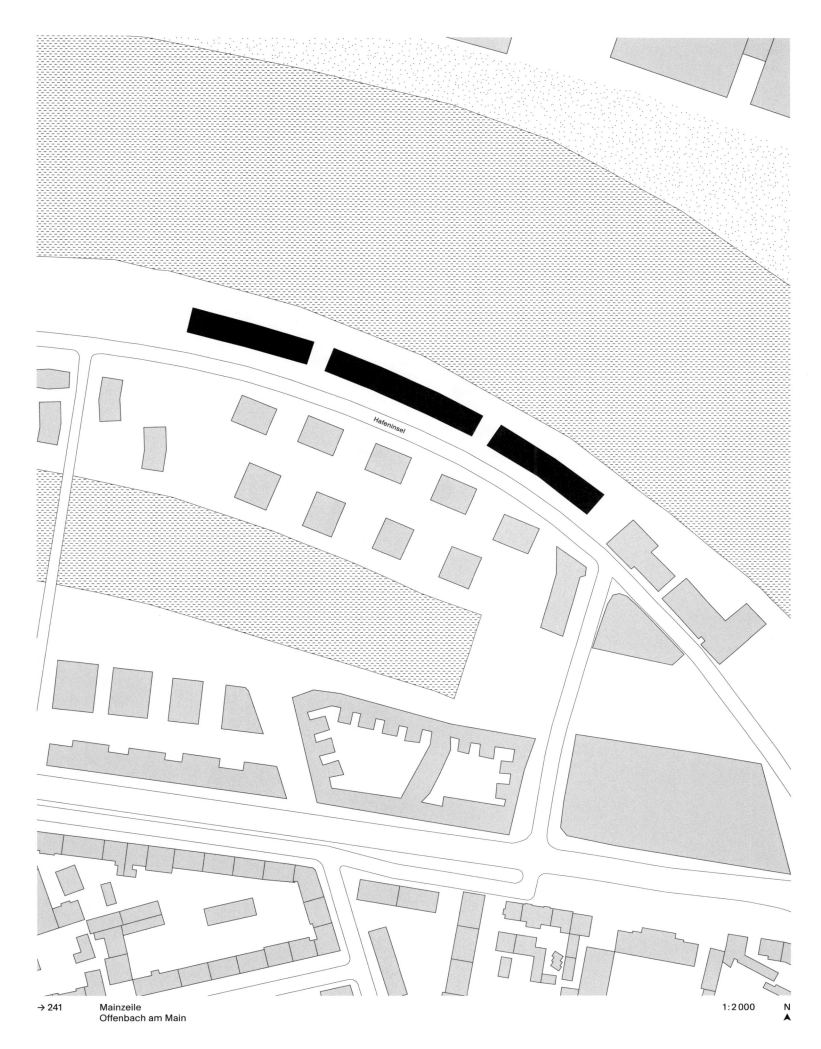

→ 241 Mainzeile
Offenbach am Main

1:2 000   N

Siedlung • Housing Estate

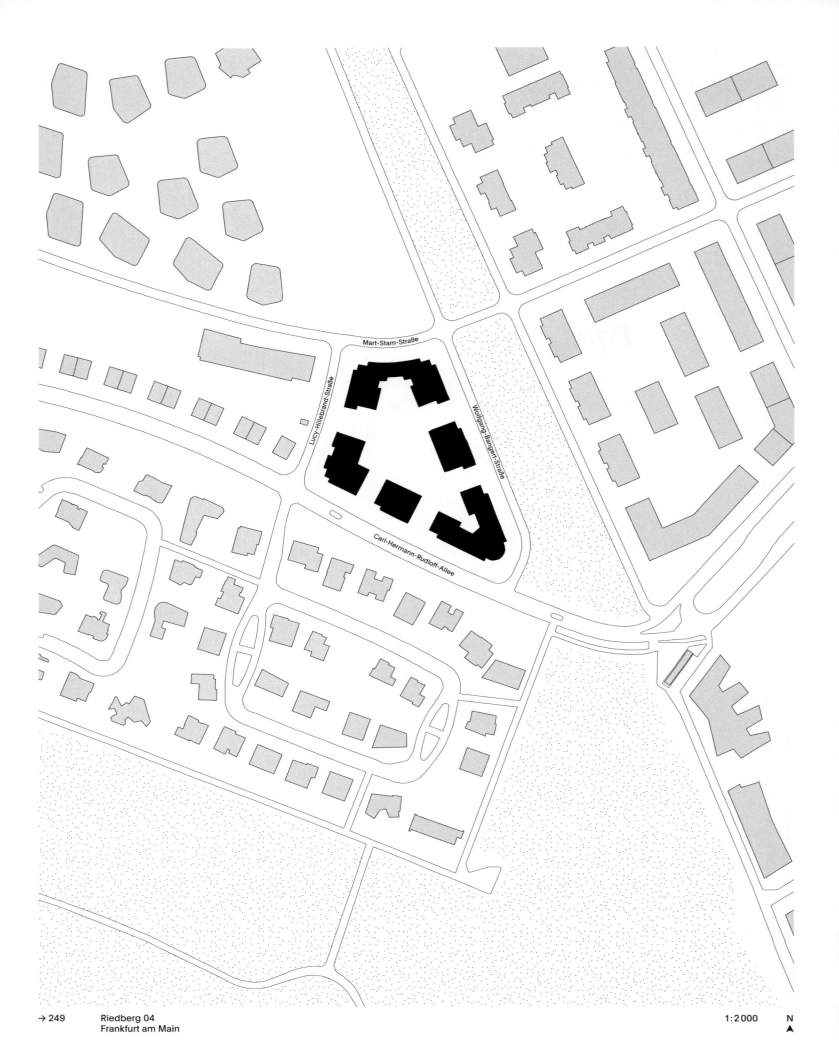

Riedberg 04
Frankfurt am Main

1:2000

2008 Wohnen im Park
Houses in the park
Frankfurt am Main

Inmitten des denkmalgeschützten Mühlbergparks auf einer Anhöhe im Südosten von Frankfurt-Sachsenhausen befinden sich die sechs Stadtvillen des Projekts »Wohnen im Park«. Die 2008 fertiggestellten, luxuriösen Wohnhäuser stehen im Kontext der Umnutzung des früheren Mühlberg-Krankenhauses: 1871 als Villa eines Offenbacher Fabrikanten gegründet, beherbergte sie seit 1936 das Krankenhaus des Diakoniewerks Bethanien. Nach der Schließung 2004 wurde das Bestandsgebäude abgebrochen und durch eine 2008 eröffnete Seniorenresidenz ersetzt. In dieser Phase ergab sich die einmalige Chance, im westlichen Teil des Areals 32 hochwertige Eigentumswohnungen in einer offenen Gruppe von sechs Baukörpern zu errichten. Der Park blieb dabei nicht nur in seiner historischen Gestalt bestehen, sondern wurde im Rahmen der Baugenehmigung auch denkmalgerecht saniert und ist weiterhin frei zugänglich. Durch die Nutzung des ehemaligen Krankenhaus-Parkplatzes als Baufläche der sechs Neubauten konnte die Grünanlage in Gänze erhalten und vollständig autofrei gestaltet werden. Der Zugang zur Tiefgarage erfolgt nun von außerhalb des Parks und wurde in die umfassende Parkmauer integriert. Um eine selbstverständliche Integration in den Park zu ermöglichen, wurden die Grünflächen um die Wohnhäuser herum nicht privatisiert.

Die städtebauliche Konzeption ist so schlicht wie effektiv: Zunächst wurden je drei Häuser in zwei Reihen angeordnet, durch deren Versatz Nischen entstehen. Die offene Gruppierung der Häuser und die raumbildende Wirkung der umlaufenden Parkmauer erzeugt ein Wechselspiel zwischen Offenheit und Geschlossenheit, Intimität und Weite. Ein Höhenversatz der beiden Reihen, die zur Straße drei, zum Park hin vier Geschosse umfasst, verstärkt die räumliche Inszenierung der Wohnanlage. Mit ihrer zurückhaltenden Gestaltung und den eleganten Proportionen erinnern die mit Klinkern in verschiedenen Brauntönen verkleideten Häuser an die frühen Wohnbauten Ludwig Mies van der Rohes, etwa die Häuser »Lange« und »Esters«. Die Großzügigkeit der Gesamtanlage setzt sich mit großformatigen Holzfenstern, den dunklen Steinbelägen der Treppenhäuser sowie hohen Wänden und Parkettböden in den Zwei- bis Fünfzimmerwohnungen auch im Inneren fort.

The "Houses in the park" is a development of six new urban villas built in the middle of Mühlbergpark, a protected park area on a hill in the southeast of the district of Sachsenhausen in Frankfurt. These luxury residences, completed in 2008, stand in the context of the conversion of the former Mühlberg Hospital, which was built originally as a villa by an Offenbach factory owner, but used from 1936 onwards as a hospital by the Diakoniewerk Bethanien. Following its closure in 2004, the hospital building was demolished and replaced by an old people's home, opened in 2008. In this phase there was a unique opportunity to build 32 high-quality freehold apartments, grouped in six openly spaced buildings, in the west of the site. The park remained, not only in its historic form, but, as part of the process of obtaining planning permission, it was also restored in keeping with its protected status, and has remained open to the public.

By using the former hospital car park as the plot for the six new buildings, the entire park was preserved and kept completely car-free. The entrance to the underground car park is now outside the park and is integrated into the perimeter wall. To ensure the villas would blend well into the park, the green spaces around them were not privatised.

The design concept behind these urban villas is as simple as it is effective: Two rows, each with three buildings, are offset against each other, creating spaces between them. This loose grouping of the volumes and the space-defining effect of the perimeter park wall gives rise to an interplay of open and closed spaces, of intimacy and expanse. Further emphasis of this spatial quality comes from the difference in height between the two rows: The row towards the street is three storeys high, the one towards the park has four storeys. With their simple, restrained design and elegant proportions, these apartment buildings, clad with clinker in various shades of brown, are reminiscent of the early villas of Mies van der Rohe, for example the Lange and Esters houses. The spaciousness of the whole complex is continued in the interior in the use of large-format wooden windows, dark stone tiles in the stairwells, high walls and parquet flooring in the two- to five-roomed apartments.

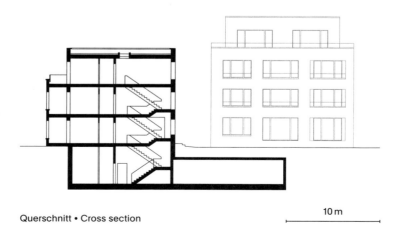

Querschnitt • Cross section   10 m

Wohnungen • Apartments: 32
Geschossfläche (BGF) • Floor area (gross): 4830 m²
Fertigstellung • Completion: 2008
Bauherr • Client: Frank Heimbau
Mitarbeit • Project team: Jelena Duchrow, Eleanor Lucke, Cristina Naranjo
Adresse • Address: Auf dem Mühlberg 30, 60599 Frankfurt am Main

← Blick über den Park nach Süden • View towards the south across the park
→ Blick nach Norden auf das Haus Am Mühlberg 30c • View towards the north of Am Mühlberg 30c

Historische Parkmauer am Hühnerweg mit Tor zur Wohnanlage • Historic park wall on Hühnerweg with gate to the residential complex

Grundriss Regelgeschoss • Standard floor plan

Mariannenstraße

N 1:500

← Blick über den Hof nach Westen auf das Haus Am Mühlberg 30c • View of Am Mühlberg 30c, looking west across the courtyard
→ Innenhof mit privater Terrasse und Blick nach Westen • Inner courtyard with private terrace and view towards the west

Siedlung • Housing Estate

Blick entlang der zum Park orientierten Ostseite der Wohnanlage • View along the east side of the residential complex facing the park

2013   **Mainzeile**
                 Offenbach am Main

Siedlung • Housing Estate

Die Transformation des ehemaligen Industriehafens zu einem neuen Quartier ist seit Mitte der 2000er-Jahre das zentrale Stadtentwicklungsvorhaben der Stadt Offenbach am Main. Mit Beginn der ersten Erschließungsarbeiten im Jahr 2009 wurde der Grundstein für das Projekt »Hafen Offenbach« gelegt: Auf dem 25,6 Hektar großen Areal nordwestlich der Innenstadt entstehen seither neue Wohnungen, Büros, Einzelhandelsflächen und öffentliche Parkanlagen wie der Untere und Obere Molenpark. Auch der Neubau der Hochschule für Gestaltung (HfG Offenbach) ist Bestandteil des Vorhabens, das sich auf zwei Areale – einen Uferstreifen und eine Insel – entlang des Mains verteilt. Als Auftakt zur Bebauung der Maininsel realisierten *Stefan Forster Architekten* 2013 für die kommunale Wohnungsbaugesellschaft *ABG Frankfurt Holding* die »Mainzeile«.

Der achtgeschossige Wohnkomplex im Passivhausstandard besteht aus drei Zeilen mit insgesamt 178 Mietwohnungen, die dem bogenförmigen Flusslauf folgen und sich über eine Länge von knapp 250 Metern zwischen den markanten Kopfbauten aufspannen. Wie diese ist die Sockelzone der gekrümmten Zeile zu beiden Seiten in rotem Kammputz ausgeführt – ein verbindendes Element, das Bezüge zum ehemaligen Industriehafen aufnimmt und die Einheit des Komplexes architektonisch sichtbar werden lässt. Zur Vernetzung des neuen Hafenviertels mit dem Mainufer wurden in jedem Bauteil zwei doppelgeschossige Durchgänge eingerichtet. Aufgrund der Lärmemissionen von Industrieanlagen auf der nördlichen Mainseite präsentiert sich die Flussseite mit einer geschlossenen Fassade; sämtliche Loggien sind durchgehend auf der Südseite angeordnet. Auch die Grundrisse der beidseitig orientierten Wohnungen folgen den rigiden Schallschutzvorgaben, sodass Nebenräume wie Küche und Bad nach Norden orientiert sind, Schlafräume und Wohnzimmer hingegen nach Süden, wo eine großzügige, durchlaufende Loggia die Aufenthaltsräume miteinander verbindet. Die Öffnung der Wohnungen zum Quartier findet im Erdgeschoss mit einer begrünten Vorgartenzone ihre Fortsetzung.

Since the mid 2000s, the City of Offenbach am Main has been engaged in a large-scale urban development project to transform a former riverside industrial area into a new residential district. When site preparation began in 2009, the foundation stone was laid for the "Hafen Offenbach" project. Since then, on this 25.6 hectare site northwest of the inner city, work has been progressing on building new apartments, offices, retail space and public parks, including the "Untere Molenpark" and the "Obere Molenpark". The new building for Offenbach's University of Art and Design (Hochschule für Gestaltung Offenbach) is also part of the project. The site is divided into two sections along the River Main: a riverside strip and an island. In 2013 the first development on the island was completed: the "Mainzeile", housing designed and built for the local-authority housing company *ABG Frankfurt Holding* by *Stefan Forster Architekten*.

This eight-storey residential complex, built to the passive house standard, consists of three linear blocks containing a total of 178 rental apartments. The blocks stretch between the two distinctive end sections in a 250-meter line along the bend of the river. Like the end sections, the base storeys of the curved block are finished with red comb rendering on both sides – a unifying element that is both a reference to the former industrial port area and an architectural signal of the unity of the complex.

To link the new district of "Hafen Offenbach" to the banks of the river, there are two double-height passageways running through each section of the building. Because of the noise emissions from industrial plant on the north bank of the Main, the river-facing side of this complex presents a closed façade; all loggias are positioned on the south side. The ground plans of the apartments facing both sides also conform to rigid acoustic insulation specifications, which means that ancillary rooms like kitchens and bathrooms face north but bedrooms and lounges face south, where generously sized, continuous loggias connect the main rooms together. On the ground floor, small front gardens continue the opening out of the apartments towards the outside.

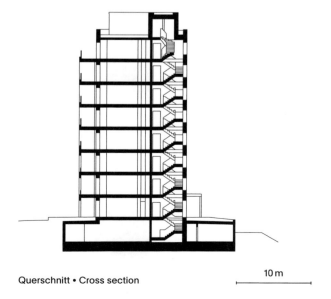

Querschnitt • Cross section   10 m

Wohnungen • Apartments: 178
Geschossfläche (BGF) • Floor area (gross): 21 540 m²
Fertigstellung • Completion: 2013
Bauherr • Client: ABG Frankfurt Holding
Mitarbeit • Project team: Ulrich Ricker, Jelena Duchrow, Christoph Ney, Wiebke Nolte
Adresse • Address: Hafeninsel 15–27, 63067 Offenbach am Main

Blick in die Hafeninsel entlang der Südseite des Gebäudes • View along Hafeninsel showing the south side of the building

Siedlung • Housing Estate

Westseite des Gebäudes am Main • West side of the building facing the river Main

Hafeninsel
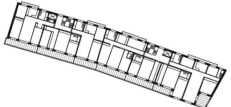

Grundriss Regelgeschoss • Standard floor plan

N 1:1200

Mainzeile

Fassadenansicht der Südseite mit Loggien • View of the façade, south side with loggias

Fassadenansicht der Südseite • Façade elevation, south side

2017 Riedberg 04
Frankfurt am Main

Das Frankfurter Neubaugebiet »Riedberg« galt lange Zeit als eines der größten Stadterweiterungsprojekte in Deutschland. Auf einer Fläche von 266 Hektar entstanden seit 1997 Wohnungen für rund 16.000 Einwohner, ein Einkaufszentrum und der neue Campus der Goethe-Universität, der insbesondere die naturwissenschaftlichen Institute und Forschungseinrichtungen sowie angegliederte *Lifescience*-Firmen aufnimmt. Mit seiner überwiegend monofunktionalen Struktur und der zumeist offenen Bauweise zeigt sich der Riedberg – trotz formaler Anleihen an den Prinzipien der »europäischen Stadt« – als klassische Siedlung in Stadtrandlage, wurde aufgrund seiner städtebaulichen Vielgestaltigkeit aber immer wieder auch Gegenstand von Kritik. Die unter Architektinnen und Architekten engagiert geführten Debatten spiegeln sich mitunter in den unterschiedlichen Entwicklungsphasen des Riedbergs wider: Während die ersten Bauabschnitte in lockerer Bebauung noch an die dörflich geprägten Nachbarstadtteile anknüpfen, nahm die Dichte seither deutlich zu.

Als siebter und letzter Abschnitt komplettiert der sogenannte »Westflügel« den Riedberg. Von der Innenstadt kommend bildet in seinem südlichen Bereich die Wohnanlage Riedberg 04 mit einem markant abgerundeten Eckhaus den Eingang in das neue Quartier. Mit ihrer offenen, aufgelockerten Bauweise folgt das Ensemble aus fünf gestaffelten Baukörpern dem städtebaulichen Rahmenplan und nimmt zugleich Elemente klassischer Blockrandstrukturen auf. So bildet die straßenbegleitende, blockhafte Artikulation der Baukörper nach außen einen eindeutig definierten Straßenraum und nach innen einen gemeinschaftlich genutzten Hof mit Grünanlage und Spielplatz, die um einen zentralen Baum herum angelegt wurden. Die Konturen der Gebäude variieren die Ecksituation und interpretieren mit ihrer profilierten Klinkerverkleidung und der plastischen Fassadengliederung das Thema »Stadtvilla« neu. Eine dem Straßenverlauf folgende Klinkermauer fasst die Anlage ein und gewährleistet die Privatheit der Bewohner. Die 106 Zwei- bis Vierzimmerwohnungen sind mit großzügigen Außenräumen in Form von Loggien und Terrassen ausgestattet und bieten einen hohen Wohnkomfort. Neben der Wohnanlage Riedberg 04 wurden in demselben Stadtteil seit 2012 noch drei weitere Anlagen von *Stefan Forster Architekten* realisiert.

For a long time the new urban district of Riedberg in Frankfurt was one of the biggest urban expansion projects in Germany. From 1997 onwards, on a site of 226 hectares in size, apartments were built for around 16,000 residents, plus a shopping centre and the new campus of Goethe University, accommodating in particular the natural sciences institutes and research facilities, along with associated life science companies. With its mainly monofunctional structure and generally open design, Riedberg, despite formal references to the principles of the "European city", presents as a classic estate on the outskirts of a city. Yet it also attracted some criticism because of the diversity of its urban architecture. Architects engaged in intensive debate about Riedberg, and this is reflected also in the different development phases on the site: In the early phases of construction a looser arrangement is evident, sensitive to the village-like character of the adjacent urban areas, while later the density of development increased considerably.

The "West Wing", as it is known, is the seventh and last section of Riedberg to be built. Seen from the city-centre side, the southern part of the Riedberg 04 residential complex, with its distinctively rounded corner building, marks the entrance to the new district. Open and spacious in design, the ensemble of five buildings of graduated height adheres to the urban master plan while also taking up elements of classic block-edge structures. The block-like articulation of the building volumes along the street create a clearly defined street space to the outside and, to the inside, a shared courtyard with green spaces and a playing area, arranged around a tree in the centre. The contours of the building enliven the corner situation, and, with their profiled clinker cladding and sculptural façade articulation, re-interpret the theme of the "urban villa". A clinker wall following the line of the street encloses the ensemble and affords privacy for the residents. 106 two- to four-roomed apartments with a generous amount of outside space in the form of loggias and terraces provide a high standard of accommodation. As well as Riedberg 04, *Stefan Forster Architekten* also built three other complexes in the same urban district since 2012.

Längsschnitt • Longitudinal section   10 m

Wohnungen • Apartments: 106
Geschossfläche (BGF) • Floor area (gross): 11 000 m²
Fertigstellung • Completion: 2017
Bauherr • Client: Swiss Life AG
Mitarbeit • Project team: Mira Sennrich, Sandra Söhnel, Daniela Vorrath, Annika Vedder, Michael Thomas, Julia Tamm
Adresse • Address: Carl-Hermann-Rudloff-Allee 6, Wolfgang-Bangert-Straße 1–3, Lucy-Hillebrand-Straße 2–4, 60483 Frankfurt am Main

Blick von Süden über die Carl-Hermann-Rudloff-Allee / Ecke Wolfgang-Bangert-Straße • View from the south across the junction of Carl-Hermann-Rudloff-Allee / Wolfgang-Bangert-Straße

Siedlung • Housing Estate

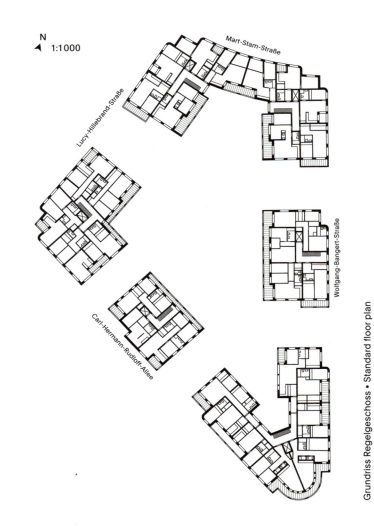

Grundriss Regelgeschoss • Standard floor plan

Blick von Nordwesten auf die Ecke Mart-Stam-Straße / Lucy-Hillebrand-Straße
View from the northwest of the junction of Mart-Stam-Straße / Lucy-Hillebrand-Straße

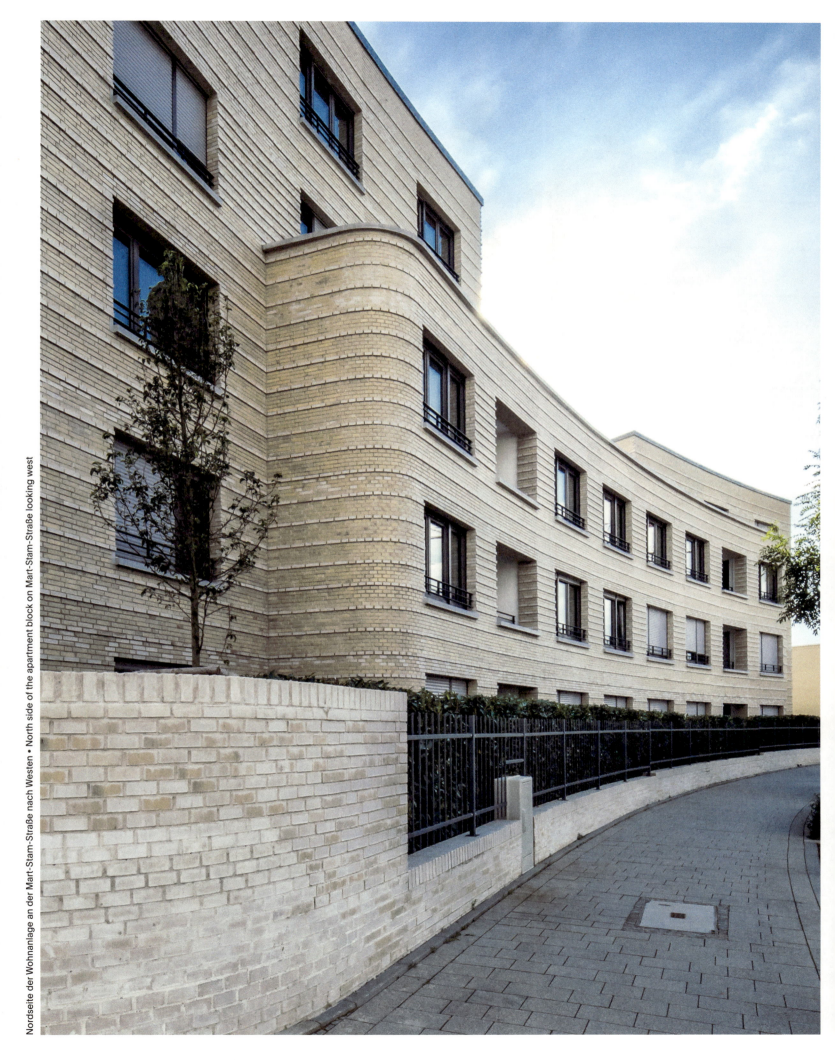

Nordseite der Wohnanlage an der Mart-Stam-Straße nach Westen • North side of the apartment block on Mart-Stam-Straße looking west

Siedlung • Housing Estate

Fassadenansicht an der Carl-Hermann-Rudloff-Allee • Façade elevation, Carl-Hermann-Rudloff-Allee

Transformation

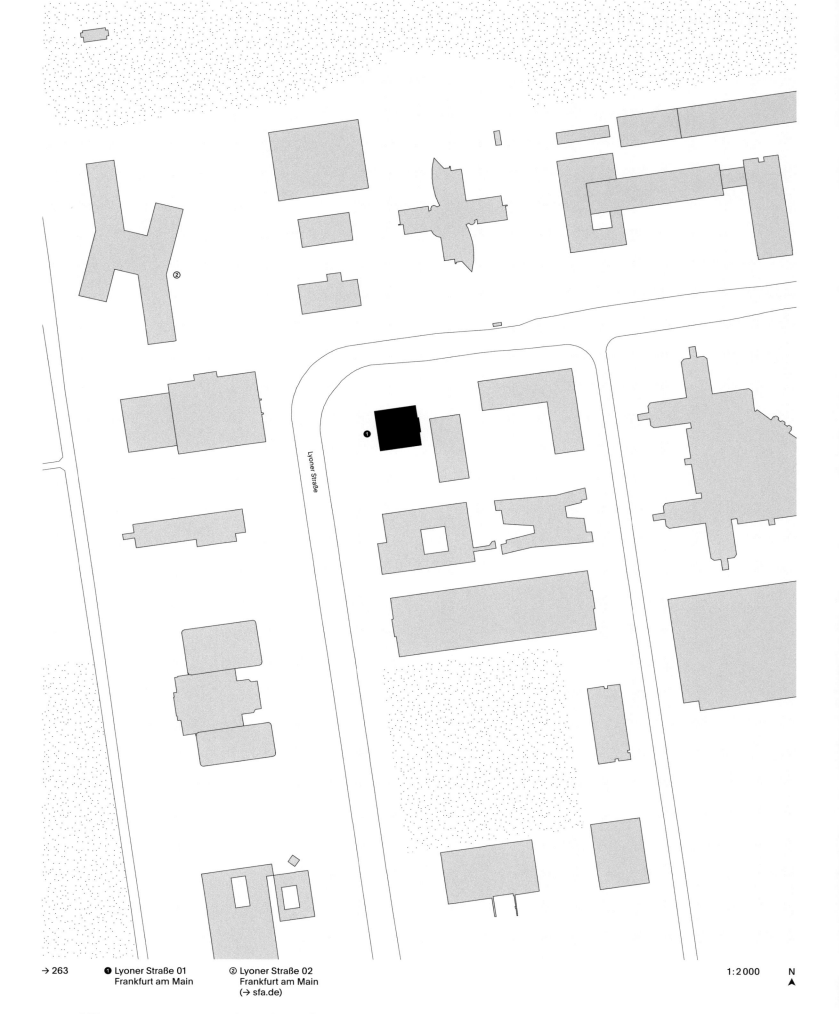

→ 263　❶ Lyoner Straße 01　② Lyoner Straße 02
　　　　　Frankfurt am Main　　Frankfurt am Main
　　　　　　　　　　　　　　　(→ sfa.de)

1:2000　N

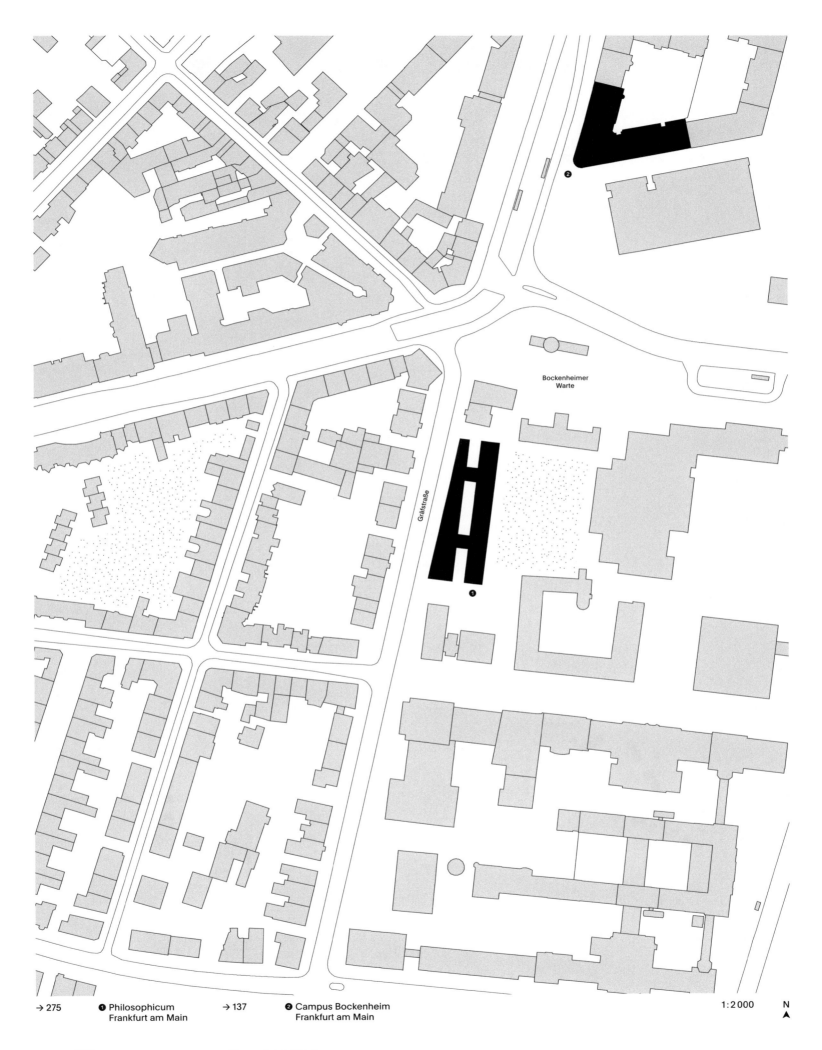

| → 275 | ❶ Philosophicum Frankfurt am Main | → 137 | ❷ Campus Bockenheim Frankfurt am Main | 1:2000 N |

Transformation

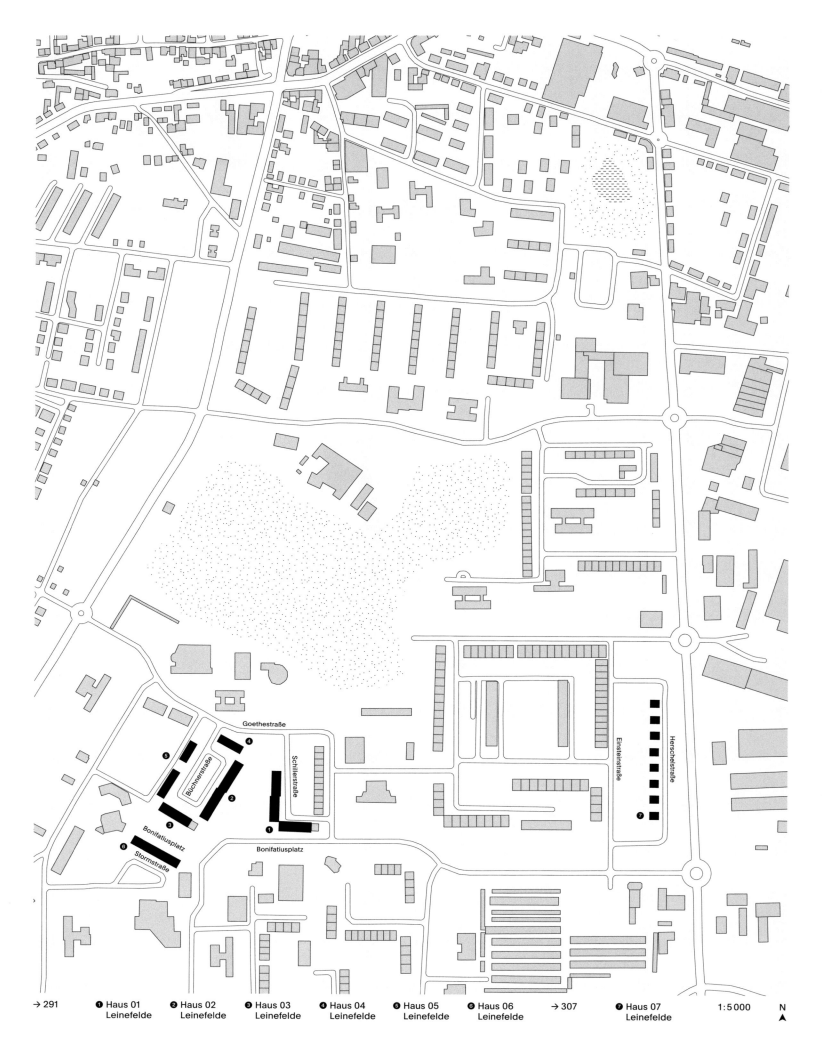

| ① Haus 01 Leinefelde | ② Haus 02 Leinefelde | ③ Haus 03 Leinefelde | ④ Haus 04 Leinefelde | ⑤ Haus 05 Leinefelde | ⑥ Haus 06 Leinefelde | ⑦ Haus 07 Leinefelde | 1:5000 | N |

Lagepläne • Site plans

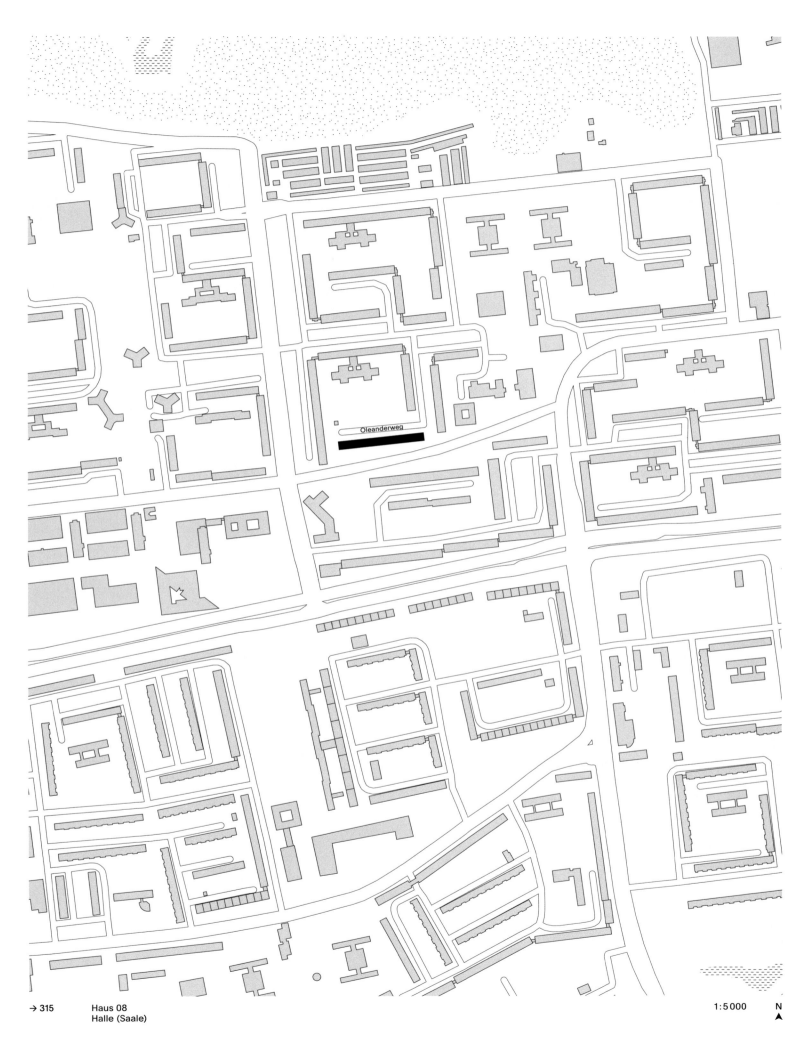

→ 315　Haus 08
　　　　Halle (Saale)

261　　　　Transformation　　　　1:5000　N

2010 Lyoner Straße 01
Frankfurt am Main

Die Bürostadt Niederrad war ein 144 Hektar großes Gewerbegebiet im Südwesten von Frankfurt. In den 1960er-Jahren nach dem stadtplanerischen Leitbild einer »Bürostadt im Grünen« entstanden, zeigten sich bereits ab den 1980er-Jahren die Schwächen ihrer rein monofunktionalen Struktur: Die einseitige Nutzung und die fehlende Vernetzung mit den benachbarten Stadtteilen und dem Zentrum führten zu einem wachsenden Leerstand, der 2006 einen Spitzenwert von 30 Prozent erreichte. Neben dem veralteten Standard der Bürobauten machte auch die Konkurrenz durch das neue, direkt am Flughafen gelegene Gewerbegebiet *Gateway Gardens* ein Umdenken erforderlich. Daher wurde als Reaktion auf die strukturellen Probleme des Stadtteils und den generellen Wohnungsmangel in Frankfurt das Konzept einer städtebaulichen Erneuerung durch partielle Umnutzung von Büros in Wohnraum entwickelt.

Ein erster Baustein der Transformation war das 2010 realisierte Wohnhochhaus in der Lyoner Straße. Drei Maßnahmen wurden kombiniert, um das aus den späten 1960er-Jahren stammende und seit geraumer Zeit leerstehende Bürogebäude zu revitalisieren: Zunächst musste das Gebäude vollständig entkernt und auf seine Tragstruktur zurückgebaut werden. Im zweiten Schritt folgte die Umwandlung in ein Wohnhaus, die durch den quadratischen Grundriss und die Entfernung von zwei Aufzügen begünstigt wurde. Nun konnten nicht nur Sanitäranlagen und sonstige Infrastruktur in den Kern verlegt, sondern auch völlig freie Wohnungsgrundrisse mit einer Staffelung vom Zwei- bis zum Siebenspänner entwickelt werden. Schließlich verlieh die Aufstockung um drei Geschosse – inklusive des abschließenden Staffelgeschosses – in Verbindung mit abgesenkten Brüstungen dem Hochhaus elegantere, gestreckte Proportionen. Die Adaption der Bürohaustypologie drückt sich derweil in der Gestalt des Gebäudes aus, das seine Herkunft nicht verleugnet und die Ästhetik der 1970er-Jahre mit der horizontal geschichteten *curtain wall*-Fassade in eine zeitgemäße, an die klassische Moderne erinnernde Bandfassade überträgt. Ein klar strukturierter Sockel, die eingeschnittenen Loggien der Eckwohnungen und das leuchtende Weiß des Baukörpers machen die funktionalen Veränderungen im Inneren nach außen sichtbar.

Mit seinen 98 Wohneinheiten entstand mit dem Wohnhochhaus Lyoner Straße 01 ein Pionierprojekt in der ehemaligen Bürostadt Niederrad, die im Zuge des Wandels zu einem gemischten Büro- und Wohnstadtteil 2017 offiziell in »Lyoner Quartier« umbenannt wurde.

Niederrad business district was a 144-hectare commercial site in the southwest of Frankfurt. It was created in the 1960s in line with the planning model of an out-of-town office development. Already by the 1980s, however, weaknesses in its purely monofunctional structure were evident: One-sided utilization and poor connections to adjacent urban districts and the city centre led to an increase in vacancies, this reaching a peak in 2006, when 30 percent of the available space stood empty. The dated standard of the office buildings, combined with competition from the new commercial district *Gateway Gardens* located right by the airport, prompted a complete re-think. In response to the structural problems of this district and in view of the housing shortage in Frankfurt, a concept was developed for urban renewal by converting offices into residential space.

A first step in the transformation was to create a residential high-rise in Lyoner Straße, completed in 2010. Three measures were combined to revitalise a late 1960s office building which had stood empty for some time. First the building was completely gutted, leaving only the load-bearing frame. Then it was transformed into a residential block, helped by the square ground plan and the removal of two lifts. This enabled the sanitary installations and other infrastructure to be located in this core, and also facilitated the development of completely flexible apartment plans with the number of apartments per floor ranging from two to seven. Finally, by extending the building upwards three storeys (including a top floor set back from the façade) and by lowering the parapets of the high-rise, slimmer, more elegant proportions were achieved. This adaptation of office-building typology is expressed in the form of the building, which does not seek to deny its origins: the 1970s aesthetic with a horizontally layered curtain wall façade is transferred into a contemporary banded façade reminiscent of the classical Modern. A clearly structured base storey, the incised loggias of the corner apartments and the glowing white of the building volume highlight the functional changes both inside and outside.

Providing 98 residential units, the Lyoner Straße 01 high-rise is a pioneering project in the former business district of Niederrad, which as part of the change to a mixed residential and office development, was officially renamed in 2017 as the "Lyoner Quartier", or Lyoner District.

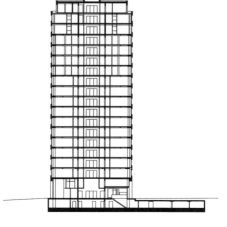

Schnitt • Section   10 m

Wohnungen • Apartments: 98
Geschossfläche (BGF) • Floor area (gross): 9 840 m²
Fertigstellung • Completion: 2010
Bauherr • Client: Dreyer Vierte Verwaltungsgesellschaft mbH
Mitarbeit • Project team: Florian Kraft, Jelena Duchrow, Andreas Wenger, Ildikó Návay, Stuart Cowie
Adresse • Address: Lyoner Straße 19, 60528 Frankfurt am Main

← Blick entlang der Lyoner Straße auf die offene Bebauungsstruktur der Bürostadt Niederrad • View along Lyoner Straße of the open development structure of Niederrad commercial district
→ Blick über die Lyoner Straße von Südwesten • View across Lyoner Straße from the southwest

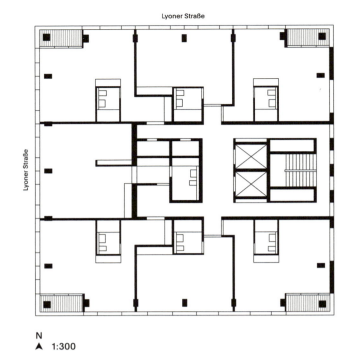

Grundriss Regelgeschoss (7-Spänner)
Standard floor plan (7 apartments)

Westseite des Gebäudes mit gewerblicher Sockelzone • West side of the building with commercial space at ground floor

270   Lyoner Straße 01

← Innenaufnahme mit Blick nach Süden auf die Bürostadt Niederrad (mit den Olivetti-Türmen von Egon Eiermann) • Interior with a view towards the south of the commercial district of Niederrad (showing the Olivetti towers of Egon Eiermann)
↓ Blick nach Südwesten über Teich und Grünflächen des Hilton-Hotels • View towards the southwest across the pond and lawns of the Hilton Hotel

Innenaufnahme des Aufzugsportals aus Baustahl • Interior, steel door to lift

2016   Philosophicum
        Frankfurt am Main

Das zwischen 1958 und 1960 von Ferdinand Kramer für die Frankfurter Goethe-Universität im Stil des Funktionalismus errichtete Philosophicum zählt zu den bedeutendsten Baudenkmälern der Nachkriegsmoderne in Frankfurt. Der Stahlskelettbau mit knapp 80 Metern Länge und 10,58 Metern Tiefe war mit seinem außenliegenden Tragsystem aus Doppel-T-Stützen, den vor der Fassade platzierten Treppenhäusern und dem stützenfreien, flexibel unterteilbaren Innenraum ein Pionierbau seiner Zeit. Dennoch war das Gebäude in der Öffentlichkeit und bei seinen Nutzerinnen und Nutzern gleichermaßen umstritten: Von der Straße abgewandt stand es isoliert im städtischen Raum; zudem führte die nur fünf Zentimeter starke *curtain wall*-Fassade zu extremen thermischen Schwankungen – so konnte es im Winter bitterkalt und im Sommer unerträglich heiß sein. 2003 wurde der einstige Sitz der philosophischen Fakultät durch den Umzug der Universität an den neuen Campus Westend aufgegeben. Es folgten mehr als zehn Jahre Leerstand, an dessen Ende der Abriss diskutiert wurde. Erst eine Projektgruppe für alternatives Wohnen brachte mit ihrem Engagement für den Erhalt die Wende – ihr Vorhaben der Umnutzung in Wohnungen scheiterte jedoch an der Finanzierung.

Schließlich erwarb die *RMW Wohnungsgesellschaft* das Gebäude und beauftragte *Stefan Forster Architekten* mit der Planung für die Transformation in ein Studierendenwohnheim mit 238 Appartements, einer Kita und einem Café. Grundgedanke des Entwurfs war neben der denkmalgerechten Sanierung und Umnutzung des Altbaus die Errichtung eines entlang der Gräfstraße verlaufenden Ergänzungsbaus, der durch die Übernahme der Bauflucht und Traufhöhe des gründerzeitlichen Blockrands eine bewusste Korrektur des Städtebaus der Nachkriegsmoderne vornimmt. Der neungeschossige Altbau überragt nun den mit Klinkern und Betonelementen zurückhaltend gestalteten Neubau um vier Geschosse und bleibt dahinter sichtbar. Beide Gebäudeteile sind durch die bestehenden Treppenhaustürme miteinander verbunden und werden über diese erschlossen. Aufgrund von massiven bauphysikalischen und statischen Mängeln konnte die charakteristische Rasterfassade nicht im Original erhalten werden, sondern wurde bis ins Detail sorgfältig rekonstruiert. Auch die Variation der Fensteraufteilung, die von Ferdinand Kramer abwechselnd zwei- und dreiteilig angelegt war, wurde beibehalten. So präsentiert sich die Parkseite des Philosophicums heute wieder im Zustand und der Anmutung der 1960er-Jahre – eine Qualität, die sich im Inneren mit handgemalten weißen Marmorierungen der Treppenstufen, dem Farbkonzept der Türen und den originalen Handläufen und Glasbausteinen fortsetzt.

The Philosophicum, built between 1958 and 1960 in the Functionalist style by Ferdinand Kramer for Frankfurt's Goethe University, is regarded as one of the most important monuments of post-war modern architecture in Frankfurt. With its reinforced concrete construction, almost 80 metres long and 10.58 metres deep, an exterior load-bearing frame of double T-sections, staircases positioned outside the façade and a column-free flexibly divisible interior space, this was a pioneering building in its time. Nevertheless the building was controversial, both among the wider public and among its users. Set back from the street, it stood isolated in the urban context; also its curtain wall façade, just 5 cm thick, led to extreme thermal variation – in winter the rooms could be bitter cold and in summer unbearably hot. In 2003, this one-time home of the faculty of philosophy was vacated when the university moved to the new Westend Campus. For over ten years the building stood empty, after which time there was talk of it being demolished. It was only when a project group for alternative forms of housing got involved that opinions shifted towards preserving the structure – however, their proposal to re-purpose the block for residential accommodation failed because of financing.

Finally the building was acquired by the housing association, *RMW Wohnungsgesellschaft*, and they commissioned *Stefan Forster Architekten* to plan for its transformation into a student hall of residence with 238 studio apartments, a children's day nursery and a café. The basic idea behind the design was to renovate and re-purpose the existing building in a way appropriate to its listed status, and to add a new block running along Gräfstraße. This new block would take up the line of the street and the eaves height of the late 19th-century block edge, in a conscious correction to the planning idea behind the post-war modern development. The nine-storey existing tower now rises up four floors above the new block, still visible behind the new block with its restrained design featuring clinker and concrete elements. Both building sections are linked to each other via the existing stair towers, which also accommodate the entrances. Although the characteristic grid-like façade could not be preserved in the original because of serious structural problems and deficits in building physics, it was carefully reconstructed in detail. Even the variation in the fenestration, which Ferdinand Kramer designed as alternately double- or triple-articulated, was retained. As a result the park-facing side of the Philosophicum presents today in the condition and appearance of the 1960s – a quality that is continued in the interior in hand-painted white marbling on the steps, the colour concept for the doors, and the original handrails and glass blocks.

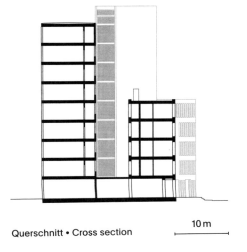

Querschnitt • Cross section   10 m

Programm • Scope: 238 Appartements, Kindertagesstätte, Café • 238 studio apartments, children's day nursery, café
Geschossfläche (BGF) • Floor area (gross): 12 130 m²
Fertigstellung • Completion: 2016
Bauherr • Client: RMW Wohnungsgesellschaft Frankfurt II GmbH
Mitarbeit • Project team: Nina Bölinger, Ildikó Návay, Nora Vitale, Anna Reeg, Wiebke Nolte, Sandra Klepsch
Adresse • Address: Gräfstraße 74–76, 60486 Frankfurt am Main

← Ostseite des Philosophicums mit Park (ehemals Campus Bockenheim) • East side of the Philosophicum with park (formerly Bockenheim Campus)
→ Blick nach Süden in die Gräfstraße mit dem Neubau (vorne) und dem Altbau (dahinter) • View towards the south down Gräfstraße with the new building (front) and the existing building (behind it)

Ostseite der Fassade mit schmaler Giebelseite • East side of the façade with narrow gable end

← Fassadenansicht des Neubaus an der Gräfstraße mit dahinterliegenden Treppentürmen des Altbaus
View of the facade of the new building on Gräfstraße with the stair towers of the existing building behind
→ Grundriss Regelgeschoss • Standard floor plan

Blick auf den Treppenturm im Innenhof zwischen Neubau (links) und Altbau (rechts)
View of the stair tower in the inner courtyard between the new building (left) and the existing building (right)

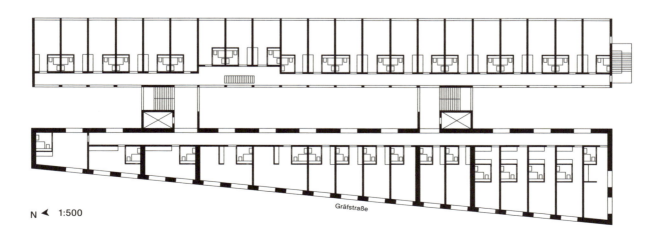

283 Transformation

Blick in den Korridor des transformierten Philosophicums • View down the corridor of the transformed Philosophicum

← Treppenhaus mit Eingang zum Altbau (Eingang zum Neubau im Rücken) • Stairwell with entrance to existing building (entrance to new building behind camera)
→ Innenaufnahme eines Studierenden-Appartements im Altbau • Interior, student apartment in the existing building

Südseite des Neubaus (links) und des Altbaus mit außenliegender Fluchttreppe (rechts) • South side of the new building (left) and of the existing building with external emergency staircase (right)

1999–2007 Haus 01–06
          Leinefelde

Inmitten des Eichsfelds im Nordwesten Thüringens liegt die Kleinstadt Leinefelde, die seit 2004 als Ortsteil zur Gemeinde Leinefelde-Worbis gehört. Infolge der deutschen Teilung war Leinefelde – damals noch ein Dorf – zum Grenzort geworden. Der Aufstieg zu einem bedeutenden Industriestandort verdankte sich dem von der DDR-Regierung 1959 beschlossenen »Eichsfeldplan« zur Modernisierung des Landkreises. Mit dem Aufbau einer großen Baumwollspinnerei in den 1960er-Jahren ging ein kontinuierlicher Wandel zur Industriestadt und ein Bevölkerungswachstum von 2.500 (1961) auf 16.500 (1986) Einwohner einher. Parallel zum Ausbau des »VEB Baumwollspinnerei« entstand mit der Südstadt ein Neubauviertel in Plattenbauweise, das vor allem den überwiegend weiblichen Textilarbeiterinnen und ihren Familien Wohnraum bieten sollte. Als das Textilkombinat nach der Wende abgewickelt wurde, geriet Leinefelde in die Krise: Der Verlust des mit Abstand größten Arbeitgebers und die wirtschaftliche Monostruktur führten zu einer massiven Abwanderung und zunehmendem Leerstand.

In Reaktion auf die desolate Lage wurde 1996 ein internationaler Architekturwettbewerb mit dem Ziel der Umstrukturierung ins Leben gerufen und Stefan Forster nach und nach mit der Transformation von sieben Plattenbauten betraut: den Häusern 01 bis 06 im Quartier Büchnerstraße sowie Haus 07 im sogenannten »Physikerviertel«. Bevor das Schlagwort vom »Stadtumbau Ost« populär wurde, galt es in Leinefelde, architektonisch-städtebauliche Strategien für eine schrumpfende Stadt zu entwickeln. Aus der Kritik an der Monotonie und städtebaulichen Vereinzelung der Plattenbauten entwickelten *Stefan Forster Architekten* das Konzept einer modernen Gartenstadt mit differenzierten Außenräumen und maßstäblich gegliederten Baukörpern.

In der ersten Phase erfolgte der teilweise Rückbau: Zunächst wurde mindestens ein Dachgeschoss entfernt, in der Regel aber zwei; lange Zeilen wurden durch den Abbruch eines Zwischensegments in zwei kompakte Baukörper geteilt (Haus 05) oder durch die Entfernung der Kopfseiten gekürzt (Haus 06). In der zweiten Phase folgte der Umbau: Nicht tragende Wände wurden entfernt, um aus den bisher standardisierten Grundrissen eine Vielzahl differenzierter Grundrisstypen entwickeln und die Bäder und Küchen mit Tageslicht versorgen zu können. Mit durchlaufenden bzw. alternierend angebrachten Balkonen erhielten die Wohnungen großzügige private Außenbereiche. Die neu geschaffenen Privatgärten der Erdgeschosswohnungen wurden vielfach in das freiraumplanerische Konzept integriert.

Mäanderförmige Klinkermauern sind ein immer wiederkehrendes gestalterisches Element bei den von Stefan Forster transformierten Plattenbauten. Als eine Art multifunktionaler Gebäudesockel differenzieren sie zwischen den öffentlichen, gemeinschaftlichen und privaten Bereichen und definieren den bisher ungefassten Straßenraum. Als Einfriedung entlang der Häuser nehmen sie die Privatgärten der Erdgeschosswohnungen auf und bilden geschützte Eingangsbereiche mit kleinen Vorplätzen aus.

Die weltweit beachtete Transformation der Plattenbauten in Leinefelde wurde unter anderem mit dem Deutschen Städtebaupreis, dem Europäischen Städtebaupreis und dem Sir-Robert-Matthew-Preis der International Union of Architects (UIA) ausgezeichnet.

In the northwest of Thuringia is the small town of Leinefelde. With the division of Germany into West and East, Leinefelde – still a village at that time – found itself very close to the border, on the GDR side. Thanks to a 1959 GDR plan to modernise the area, the town rose to become an important industrial location. A large-scale state-owned cotton spinning mill was opened there in the 1960s, and the industrial base expanded continuously, with the population growing from 2,500 (1961) to 16,500 (1986). At the same time a new prefabricated housing development was also constructed in the south of the town. This offered accommodation to the mainly female textile-industry employees and their families. After the collapse of the GDR, the textile collective was closed down and Leinefelde experienced a serious downturn. The loss of by far the largest employer in the town and the economic monostructure prompted a mass exodus of people, and as a result many empty apartments.

In 1996, as a reaction to this desperate situation, an international architectural competition was launched as part of a wider restructuring initiative. Stefan Forster Architekten received a succession of commissions to transform seven of the prefabricated high-rise blocks: Houses 01 to 06 in the Büchnerstraße district, and House 07, in the "Physicists District". Before the idea of regenerating towns in the east took hold, Leinefelde was thus already engaged with the development of architectural and planning strategies for a shrinking town. Responding to the criticism of the monotony and the urban isolation of the old panel-system buildings, Stefan Forster Architekten developed the concept of a modern garden city with a variety of differently designed open spaces and appropriately scaled and articulated building volumes.

The first phase involved partial dismantling – at least one top floor was removed, generally however two. Long linear blocks were divided into two compact volumes (House 05) by taking out an intermediate segment, or they were shortened at the ends (House 06). The second phase focused on remodelling: Non-supporting walls were removed in order to develop a range of different floor plans out of the previous standardised layouts, and to bring daylight into bathrooms and kitchens. Continuous, or alternating balconies afforded the apartments generously sized private outside space. The newly created private gardens of the ground-floor apartments were in many cases integrated into the planning concept for the open spaces.

Boundary walls of clinker brick are a recurring design element in the panel-system housing transformed by Stefan Forster. As a kind of multifunctional baseline for the building, they differentiate between the public, shared space and the private areas, and define the previously borderless street space. As a boundary wall around the buildings, they enclose the private gardens and form protected entrance areas with small forecourts.

This project to transform the panel-system residential blocks in Leinefelde attracted worldwide attention as well as a number of awards, among them the Deutscher Städtebaupreis, the European Urban & Regional Planning Award and the Sir Robert Matthew Award of the International Union of Architects (UIA).

Programm • Scope: Umbau Wohnungen: 352 / Rückbau Wohnungen: 196 • Apartments refurbished: 352 / Apartments removed: 196
Geschossfläche (BGF) • Floor area (gross): 21630 m^2
Fertigstellung • Completion: 1999–2007
Bauherr • Client: LWG Leinefelder Wohnungsbau-Genossenschaft eG
Mitarbeit • Project team: Anna Bader-Hardt, Pamela Freymüller, Julia Goldschmidt, Reinhardt Mayer, Cristina Naranjo, Helmut Pfeiffer
Adresse • Address: Schillerstraße 10–32 (Haus 01), Büchnerstraße 26–40 (Haus 02), Büchnerstraße 18–24 (Haus 03), Büchnerstraße 42–44 (Haus 04), Büchnerstraße 2–16 (Haus 05), Stormstraße 14–28 (Haus 06); 37327 Leinefelde-Worbis

Blick über den Bonifatiusplatz auf die Südseite von Haus 01 • View over Bonifatiusplatz to the south side of House 01

Westseite des Gebäudes an der Büchnerstraße • West side of the building on Büchnerstraße

Fassadenansicht der Ostseite mit Mietergärten und Loggien • View of the façade on the east side with tenant gardens and loggias

Fassadendetails der Südseite am Bonifatiusplatz • Façade details on the south side on Bonifatiusplatz

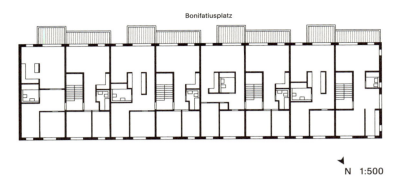

Grundriss Regelgeschoss (Haus 03) · Standard floor plan (House 03)

Bonifatiusplatz

N 1:500

Südseite des Gebäudes am Bonifatiusplatz · South side of the building on Bonifatiusplatz

Transformation

Blick von Südosten auf Haus 02 (links) und Haus 04 (rechts) • View from the southeast of House 02 (left) and House 04 (right)

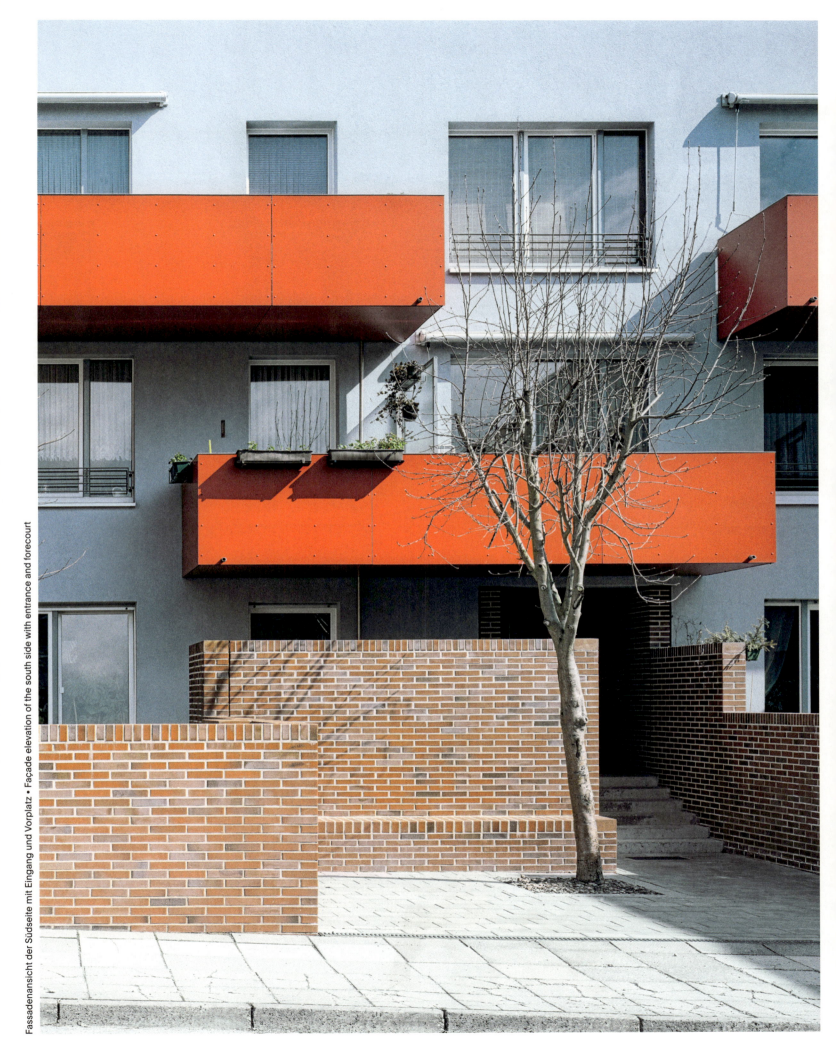

Fassadenansicht der Südseite mit Eingang und Vorplatz • Façade elevation of the south side with entrance and forecourt

Fassadenansicht mit Eingang an der Büchnerstraße • Façade elevation with entrance on Büchnerstraße

Grundriss Dachgeschoss (Haus 05)
Top floor plan (House 05)

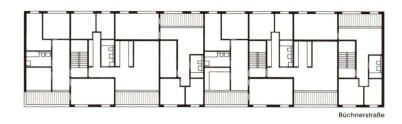

Büchnerstraße

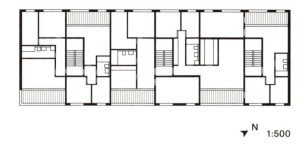

N 1:500

Blick über die Büchnerstraße nach Südwesten (im Hintergrund die Bonifatiuskirche)
View down Büchnerstraße towards the southwest (in the background Bonifatius Church)

303   Transformation

Blick entlang der Südseite des Gebäudes nach Osten • View along the south side of the building towards the east

Blick nach Westen mit den Treppen zu Bonifatiusplatz und Bonifatiuskirche (rechts im Bild)
View towards the west with the steps to Bonifatiusplatz and Bonifatius Church (right in the picture)

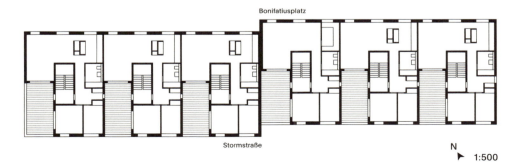
Grundriss 2. OG (Haus 06)
Plan of second floor (House 06)

305 Transformation

Fassadendetails an der Stormstraße • Façade details on Stormstraße

2004 Haus 07
Leinefelde

Als prominentestes und möglicherweise radikalstes Beispiel für den Stadtumbau in Leinefelde kann die Transformation einer 180 Meter langen Plattenbauzeile im »Physikerviertel«, dem östlichen Teil der Leinefelder Südstadt, gelten. Die Entwurfsstrategie sah die Kombination unterschiedlicher Maßnahmen vor: Zunächst wurden Zwischensegmente in regelmäßigen Abständen aus dem Volumen des Plattenbaus geschnitten und acht freistehende Häuser geschaffen, die wiederum um jeweils ein Geschoss gekürzt wurden. Mit der »Stadtvilla«, einem solitären, kleinen Geschosswohnungsbau auf quadratischem Grundriss, entstand ein neuer Bautypus. Der Umbau von Haus 07 folgte dem Gedanken einer Vermittlung zwischen der »kollektiven« Großform des Plattenbaus und der Figur des individuellen Einzelhauses. Eine durchlaufende Erdgeschosswand verbindet die acht Punkthäuser an der Ostseite miteinander und erzeugt die Anmutung einer Stadtmauer. Die Differenzierung zwischen dem Innen und Außen der Siedlung wird durch die Farbgebung akzentuiert: hier ein sachliches Grau, dort ein warmes Gelb. Der Farbwechsel an den Gebäudekanten erzeugt lebendige Kontraste. So wird der Stadteingang geografisch und der städtebauliche Neubeginn symbolisch markiert.

Im Inneren wurden die Häuser umfangreich modernisiert. Auf der Grundlage von Bewohnerbefragungen entwickelte Stefan Forster fünf unterschiedliche Grundrissvarianten aus den standardisierten Dreiraumwohnungen der »Wohnbaureihe Erfurt« von 1964, die für etwa die Hälfte der Plattenbauten in Leinefelde stand. Die ehemals innen liegenden Küchen und Bäder erhielten nun direktes Tageslicht, die Fenster wurden vergrößert und die Süd- und Westseiten mit alternierend angeordneten Balkonen mit einer Tiefe von 1,80 Meter ausgestattet. Zugunsten der plastischen Ausformulierung der Baukörper wurde auf die Sichtbarkeit unterschiedlicher Fassadenmaterialien verzichtet. Die Geländeaufschüttung auf der Westseite ermöglichte den bodengleichen Zugang der Erdgeschosswohnungen zu den neu geschaffenen Mietergärten. Durch die leicht veränderte Topografie und die Ausrichtung der Häuser zum Innenbereich der Siedlung konnte auch die Erschließung von der Ost- an die Westseite verlegt werden.

Die Transformation von Haus 07 steht exemplarisch für die Strategie, alte Bausubstanz zu erhalten und den Strukturwandel als Chance für eine qualitative, an den Prinzipien der Gartenstadt angelehnte Erneuerung des Siedlungsbaus zu sehen.

The most prominent and possibly the most radical example of urban redevelopment in Leinefelde is the transformation of a 180-metre precast concrete panel system building ("*Plattenbau*"), in the "Physicists District" in the eastern part of Leinefelde-Südstadt. The strategy behind this design proposal involved a combination of different measures: First intermediate segments were cut out at regular intervals along the line of the block to leave eight separate "houses", the top floors of which were removed. A new type of building was thus created – the "urban villa", a solitaire, small apartment block on a square ground plan. The redevelopment of House 07 pursues the idea of mediating between the "collective" large form of the panel-system block and the shape of the individual, free-standing house. A continuous wall links the eight volumes on the east side at ground-floor level, giving the impression of a town wall. The inward and outward faces of the estate are differentiated and accentuated by colour: a plain grey or a warm yellow. The change of colour at the corners of the buildings generates lively contrasts. House 07 not only marks the entrance to the town on this side, it is also a physical symbol of urban regeneration.

The interior of the building was extensively modernised. Based on surveys among the residents, Stefan Forster developed five different floor plans out of the standardised three-room layouts from the 1964 "Erfurt Series", which had accounted for around half of the housing blocks in Leinefelde. The kitchens and bathrooms, originally enclosed internally within the floor plan, now had daylight, larger windows were fitted and alternating balconies, 1.80 m deep, were added on the south and west sides. The emphasis in the visual face of the buildings is on the structural modelling of the volumes, rather than the materials used on the facades. Raising the level of the ground on the west side afforded level access from the ground-floor apartments to the newly created tenant gardens. Through this minor change to the topography and by orienting the blocks towards the interior of the estate, it was then possible to move the main entrances from the east to the west side.

The transformation of House 07 stands as a model for the strategy of retaining old building substance and seeing structural change as an opportunity to bring about quality regeneration of estate housing, guided by the principles of the garden city.

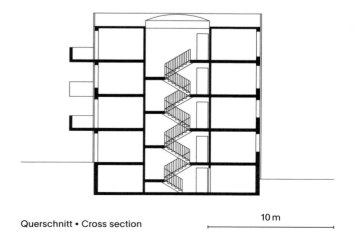

Querschnitt • Cross section — 10 m

Programm • Scope: Umbau Wohnungen: 150 / Rückbau Wohnungen: 90 •
Apartments refurbished: 150 / Apartments removed: 90
Geschossfläche (BGF) • Floor area (gross): 4 200 m²
Fertigstellung • Completion: 2004
Bauherr • Client: WVL Wohnungsbau-Verwaltungs-GmbH Leinefelde
Mitarbeit • Project team: Nikolaus Neufeld, Reinhardt Mayer
Adresse • Address: Einsteinstraße 1–15, 37327 Leinefelde-Worbis

Blick entlang der Ostseite von Haus 07 an der Herschelstraße • View along the east side of House 07 on Herschelstraße

Zugang zu den Häusern Einsteinstraße 11 und 13 von Westen • Access to the houses at Einsteinstraße 11 and 13 from the west

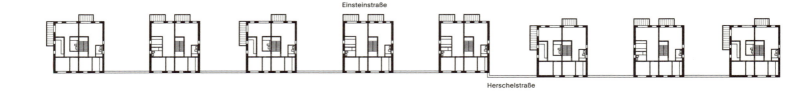

Grundriss 1. OG
Plan of first floor

N 1:1000

Blick in die Herschelstraße von Süden • View of Herschelstraße from the south

Transformation

Fassadendetails an der Herschelstraße • Façade details on Herschelstraße

Eingangsbereich von Haus 08 am Oleanderweg (mit Einfriedung) • Entrance area of House 08 on Oleanderweg (with perimeter wall)

Südseite des Gebäudes mit Mietergärten und Loggien • South side of the building with tenant gardens and loggias

Hausgrundrisse
Floor plans
1:200

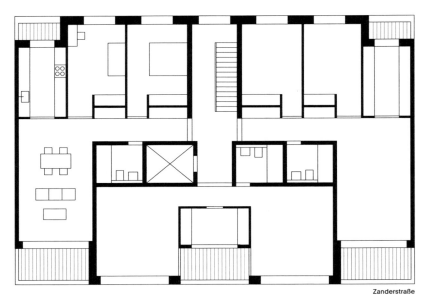

Westgarten 01, Frankfurt am Main → 113
Grundriss Regelgeschoss • Standard floor plan

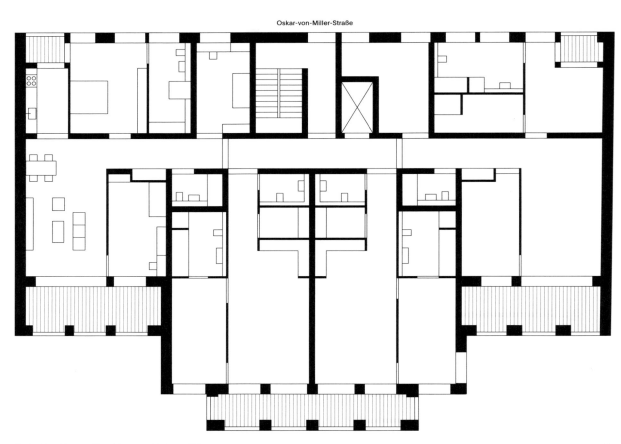

Oskar Residence, Frankfurt am Main → 125
Grundriss Regelgeschoss (Wohnhaus) • Standard floor plan (apartment block)

Hausgrundrisse • Floor plans 1:200

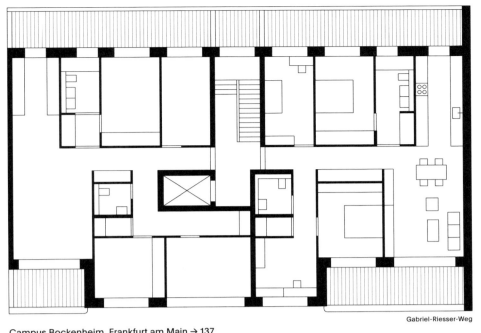

Campus Bockenheim, Frankfurt am Main → 137
Grundriss Regelgeschoss • Standard floor plan

Gabriel-Riesser-Weg

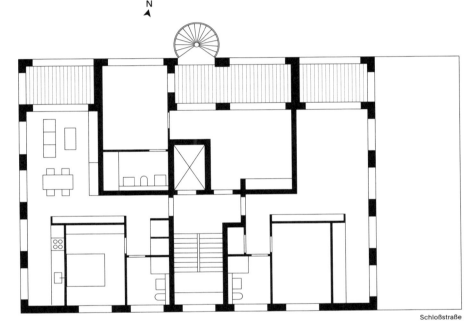

Schloßstraße, Frankfurt am Main → 149
Grundriss Regelgeschoss • Standard floor plan

Schloßstraße

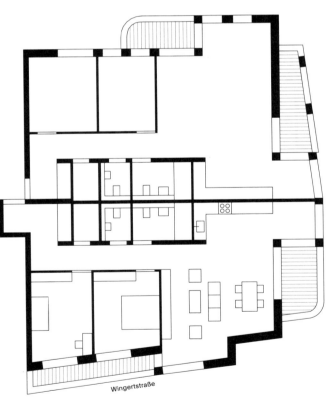

Wingertstraße

Sandweg, Frankfurt am Main → 161
Grundriss Regelgeschoss • Standard floor plan

327 Hausgrundrisse • Floor plans 1:200

331 Hausgrundrisse • Floor plans 1:200

Das Büro *Stefan Forster Architekten* wurde 1989 als Einzelgesellschaft in Darmstadt gegründet und ist seit 1995 in Frankfurt am Main ansässig. Mit rund 60 angestellten Architektinnen und Architekten hat es sich auf großstädtischen Wohnungsbau, Stadtumbau und Transformation spezialisiert. Zu den Kunden zählen neben kommunalen Wohnungsbaugesellschaften und Genossenschaften auch private Investoren und Bauträger. 2013 erfolgte die Umwandlung zur *Stefan Forster Architekten GmbH* mit den Geschäftsführern Stefan Forster, Florian Kraft und Jelena Duchrow. 2019 wurde das Büro *Stefan Forster GmbH* mit den Geschäftsführern Stefan Forster und Florian Kraft gegründet, das auf digitale Prozesse spezialisiert ist. 2018 gründeten Stefan Forster und Florian Kraft zusammen mit Torben Wadlinger die Schwestergesellschaft »Compendium BIM + Kybernetik GmbH & Co. KG«, die auf digitales Projektmanagement und digitale Prozesssteuerung spezialisiert ist.

The architectural practice *Stefan Forster Architekten* was founded in 1989 in Darmstadt as a sole proprietorship. In 1995 it moved to Frankfurt am Main. Employing a team of around 60 architects, the practice specialises in urban housing construction, urban regeneration and transformation. The clients include municipal housing associations and cooperatives, as well as private investors and developers. In 2013 the practice became *Stefan Forster Architekten GmbH* with the managing directors Stefan Forster, Florian Kraft and Jelena Duchrow. In 2019 *Stefan Forster GmbH* was founded with the managing directors Stefan Forster and Florian Kraft; this practice specialises in digital processes. In addition, in 2018, Stefan Forster and Florian Kraft, together with Torben Wadlinger, founded the sister company "Compendium BIM + Kybernetik GmbH & Co. KG", which specialises in digital project management and digital process control.

Stefan Forster

Dipl.-Ing. Architekt, geboren 1958 in Rockenhausen, gründete das Büro *Stefan Forster Architekten* 1989 in Darmstadt. Er studierte Architektur in Berlin und Venedig und war – nach ersten beruflichen Stationen in Berlin und Mannheim – von 1988 bis 1993 wissenschaftlicher Mitarbeiter am Lehrstuhl für Wohnungsbau der TU Darmstadt.

Architect, Dipl.-Ing., born in 1958 in Rockenhausen, founded the architectural practice *Stefan Forster Architekten* in 1989 in Darmstadt. He studied architecture in Berlin and Venice and, following initial experience in Berlin and Mannheim, worked as a research assistant at the Department of Housing Construction at the Technical University of Darmstadt from 1988 to 1993.

Florian Kraft

Dipl.-Ing. Architekt, geboren 1975 in Regensburg, ist seit 2013 Partner und geschäftsführender Gesellschafter. Im Anschluss an eine Lehre als Zimmermann studierte er Architektur in Dresden und Istanbul. Seit 2003 ist er für *Stefan Forster Architekten* tätig.

Architect, Dipl.-Ing., born in 1975 in Regensburg, has been a partner and managing partner since 2013. Following an apprenticeship in carpentry, he studied architecture in Dresden and Istanbul. He has been working at *Stefan Forster Architekten* since 2003.

ab • from 2025

Hagener Straße
Programm • Scope: 175 Wohnungen, Kita • 175 apartments, nursery school
Ort • Location: Düsseldorf
Geschossfläche (BGF) •
Floor area (gross): 19 030 m²
Bauherr • Client: WOGEDO Düsseldorf

Gabelsberger Block
Programm • Scope: 119 Wohnungen, Kita • 119 apartments, nursery school
Ort • Location: Aschaffenburg
Geschossfläche (BGF) •
Floor area (gross): 12 000 m²
Bauherr • Client: Stadtbau Aschaffenburg GmbH

ab • from 2023

Anwandeweg
Programm • Scope: 124 Wohnungen, Gewerbe • 124 apartments, commercial units
Ort • Location: Aschaffenburg
Geschossfläche (BGF) •
Floor area (gross): 13 500 m²
Bauherr • Client: Stadtbau Aschaffenburg GmbH

Feldstraße
Programm • Scope:
191 Wohnungen • 191 apartments
Ort • Location: Offenbach am Main
Geschossfläche (BGF) •
Floor area (gross): 21 800 m²
Bauherr • Client: Mainterra GmbH

Kleyerstraße
Programm • Scope: 398 Wohnungen, Gewerbe, Kita • 398 apartments, commercial units, nursery school
Ort • Location: Frankfurt am Main
Geschossfläche (BGF) •
Floor area (gross): 32 400 m²
Bauherr • Client: Corpus Sireo

Ludwigs-Quartier
Programm • Scope: 550 Wohnungen, Läden, Gewerbe • 550 apartments, shops, commercial units
Ort • Location: Ludwigshafen am Rhein
Geschossfläche (BGF) •
Floor area (gross): 69 000 m²
Bauherr • Client: A+G Ludwigs Quartier Gmbh & Co. KG

Platensiedlung
Programm • Scope: 684 Wohnungen, 2 Kitas, Läden, Gemeinschaftseinrichtungen • 684 apartments, 2 nursery schools, shops, community facilities
Ort • Location: Frankfurt am Main
Geschossfläche (BGF) •
Floor area (gross): 59 100 m²
Bauherr • Client: ABG Frankfurt Holding

Russland 03
Programm • Scope: 300 Wohnungen, Gewerbe • 300 apartments, commercial units
Ort • Location: Jekaterinburg
Geschossfläche (BGF) •
Floor area (gross): 27 500 m²
Bauherr • Client: Brusnika

Russland 04
Programm • Scope: 420 Wohnungen, Gewerbe • 420 apartments, commercial units
Ort • Location: Nowosibirsk
Geschossfläche (BGF) • Floor area (gross): 38 000 m²
Bauherr • Client: Brusnika

ab • from 2022

Lyoner Straße 02
Programm • Scope: 435 Wohnungen, Gewerbe • 435 apartments, commercial units
Ort • Location: Frankfurt am Main

Geschossfläche (BGF) •
Floor area (gross): 30 750 m²
Bauherr • Client: Eurohaus Frankfurt AG

MiKa
Programm • Scope: 68 Wohnungen, Gewerbe • 68 apartments, commercial units
Ort • Location: Dresden
Geschossfläche (BGF) •
Floor area (gross): 6 960 m²
Bauherr • Client: Townscape One Development GmbH & Co. KG

Russland 01
Programm • Scope:
310 Wohnungen • 310 apartments
Ort • Location: Jekaterinburg
Geschossfläche (BGF) •
Floor area (gross): 27 500 m²
Bauherr • Client: Brusnika

Überseestadt
Programm • Scope: 156 Wohnungen, Gewerbe • 156 apartments, commercial units
Ort • Location: Bremen
Geschossfläche (BGF) •
Floor area (gross): 14 160 m²
Bauherr • Client: Zechbau Bremen

Fronhofquartier
Programm • Scope: 45 Wohnungen, Gewerbe, Gastronomie • 45 apartments, commercial units, gastronomy
Ort • Location: Hanau
Geschossfläche (BGF) •
Floor area (gross): 9 000 m²
Bauherr • Client: Baugesellschaft Hanau GmbH/Terramag

Schwedler-Carré 02
Programm • Scope: 116 Wohnungen, Kita • 116 apartments, nursery school
Ort • Location: Frankfurt am Main
Geschossfläche (BGF) •
Floor area (gross): 12 260 m²
Bauherr • Client: Max Baum Immobilien GmbH

Schwedler-Carré 03
Programm • Scope:
208 Wohnungen • 208 apartments
Ort • Location: Frankfurt am Main
Geschossfläche (BGF) •
Floor area (gross): 15 620 m²
Bauherr • Client: ISARIA Objekt Schwedler Trio GmbH

Hannover 04
Programm • Scope: 83 Wohnungen, 24 Townhouses • 83 apartments, 24 townhouses
Ort • Location: Hannover
Geschossfläche (BGF) •
Floor area (gross): 12 400 m²
Bauherr • Client: GWH Wohnungsgesellschaft mbH Hessen

Hannover 05
Programm • Scope: 32 Wohnungen, Läden • 32 apartments, shops
Ort • Location: Hannover
Geschossfläche (BGF) •
Floor area (gross): 2 670 m²
Bauherr • Client: PBA ProjektBau ALSTERUFER Entwicklungs-GmbH

Paul-von-Denis-Straße
Programm • Scope: 100 Appartements (76 für Studierende), Gewerbe • 100 studio apartments (76 for students), commercial units
Ort • Location: Landau
Geschossfläche (BGF) •
Floor area (gross): 4 470 m²
Bauherr • Client: Reuter Real Estate

Hermelinweg
Programm • Scope:
42 Wohnungen • 42 apartments
Ort • Location: Bad Nauheim

Geschossfläche (BGF) •
Floor area (gross): 4 350 m²
Bauherr • Client: GeRo Real Estate

Mercedes-Areal
Programm • Scope: 119 Wohnungen, Kita • 119 apartments, nursery school
Ort • Location: Frankfurt am Main
Geschossfläche (BGF) •
Floor area (gross): 13 300 m²
Bauherr • Client: ABG Frankfurt Holding

ab • from 2021

Adolfstraße
Programm • Scope: 130 Wohnungen, Kita • 130 apartments, nursery school
Ort • Location: Hannover
Geschossfläche (BGF) •
Floor area (gross): 16 780 m²
Bauherr • Client: Projektgesellschaft Adolfstraße GmbH & Co.KG

Franklin
Programm • Scope:
155 Wohnungen • 155 apartments
Ort • Location: Mannheim
Geschossfläche (BGF) •
Floor area (gross): 14 940 m²
Bauherr • Client: GWH Bauprojekte GmbH

Hannover 03
Programm • Scope: 50 Wohnungen, Gewerbe • 50 apartments, commercial units
Ort • Location: Hannover
Geschossfläche (BGF) •
Floor area (gross): 5 500 m²
Bauherr • Client: hanova Wohnen Gmbh

Lameygarten
Programm • Scope:
17 Wohnungen • 17 apartments
Ort • Location: Mannheim
Geschossfläche (BGF) •
Floor area (gross): 2 200 m²
Bauherr • Client: Baugenossenschaft Spar- und Bauverein 1895 Mannheim eG

Mainzer Landstraße
Programm • Scope: 117 Wohnungen, Gastronomie • 117 apartments, gastronomy
Ort • Location: Frankfurt am Main
Geschossfläche (BGF) •
Floor area (gross): 5 480 m²
Bauherr • Client: HGG Dritte Projektgesellschaft mbH & Co. KG

Russland 02
Programm • Scope:
254 Wohnungen • 254 apartments
Ort • Location: Tjumen
Geschossfläche (BGF) •
Floor area (gross): 22 500 m²
Bauherr • Client: Brusnika

2020

Clouth-Quartier
Programm • Scope:
77 Wohnungen • 77 apartments
Ort • Location: Köln
Geschossfläche (BGF) •
Floor area (gross): 7 940 m²
Bauherr • Client: moderne stadt GmbH

Kalbach
Programm • Scope:
22 Wohnungen • 22 apartments
Ort • Location: Frankfurt am Main
Geschossfläche (BGF) •
Floor area (gross): 3 290 m²
Bauherr • Client: privat

Leonardo-da-Vinci-Allee
Programm • Scope: 121 Wohnungen, Kita • 121 apartments, nursery school
Ort • Location: Frankfurt am Main

Geschossfläche (BGF) •
Floor area (gross): 13 460 m²
Bauherr • Client: Instone Real Estate Development GmbH

Lindenauer Hafen
Programm • Scope:
38 Wohnungen • 38 apartments
Ort • Location: Leipzig
Geschossfläche (BGF) •
Floor area (gross): 4 670 m²
Bauherr • Client: Deutsche Wohnen AG

Lyoner Straße 03
Programm • Scope: 1
150 Wohnungen • 150 apartments
Ort • Location: Frankfurt am Main
Geschossfläche (BGF) •
Floor area (gross): 13 320 m²
Bauherr • Client: GWH Wohnungsgesellschaft mbH Hessen

Philipp-Reis-Straße
Programm • Scope:
70 Wohnungen • 70 apartments
Ort • Location: Hanau
Geschossfläche (BGF) •
Floor area (gross): 8 560 m²
Bauherr • Client: Baugesellschaft Hanau GmbH

Sonnemannstraße
Programm • Scope: 29 Wohnungen, Gewerbe • 29 apartments, commercial unit
Ort • Location: Frankfurt am Main
Geschossfläche (BGF) •
Floor area (gross): 5 020 m²
Bauherr • Client: Quartier East GmbH

2018

Schloßstraße
Programm • Scope: 13 Wohnungen, Kinderladen • 13 apartments, nursery school
Ort • Location: Frankfurt am Main
Geschossfläche (BGF) •
Floor area (gross): 1 600 m²
Bauherr • Client: Goldman/Weiner GbR
→ 149

2017

Lautenschlägerstraße
Programm • Scope:
24 Wohnungen • 24 apartments
Ort • Location: Aschaffenburg
Geschossfläche (BGF) •
Floor area (gross): 2 650 m²
Bauherr • Client: Stadtbau Aschaffenburg GmbH

Markgrafenkarree
Programm • Scope: 129 Wohnungen, Läden, Gewerbe • 129 apartments, shops, commercial units
Ort • Location: Berlin
Geschossfläche (BGF) •
Floor area (gross): 12 380 m²
Bauherr • Client: Gold.Stein Real Estate M+E GmbH & Co. KG
→ 85

Unterrather Straße
Programm • Scope:
62 Wohnungen • 62 apartments
Ort • Location: Düsseldorf
Geschossfläche (BGF) •
Floor area (gross): 7 270 m²
Bauherr • Client: Wohnungsgenossenschaft Düsseldorf-Ost eG
→ 209

Eulengasse
Programm • Scope:
26 Wohnungen • 26 apartments
Ort • Location: Frankfurt am Main
Geschossfläche (BGF) •
Floor area (gross): 4 030 m²
Bauherr • Client: ABG Frankfurt Holding/Mainterra Immobilien GmbH

Hermann-Wendel-Straße
Programm • Scope:
36 Wohnungen • 36 apartments
Ort • Location: Frankfurt am Main
Geschossfläche (BGF) •
Floor area (gross): 4 400 m²
Bauherr • Client: Cityraum Development GmbH & Co. KG/Jöckel Projektentwicklung GmbH

Oskar Residence
Programm • Scope: 28 Wohnungen, 70 Appartements, Gastronomie •
28 freehold apartments, 70 serviced apartments, gastronomy
Ort • Location: Frankfurt am Main
Geschossfläche (BGF) •
Floor area (gross): 8 810 m²
Bauherr • Client: Oskar Grundbesitz GmbH & Co. KG
→ 125

Riedberg 02
Programm • Scope:
160 Wohnungen • 160 apartments
Ort • Location: Frankfurt am Main
Geschossfläche (BGF) •
Floor area (gross): 17 160 m²
Bauherr • Client: Nassauische Heimstätte

Riedberg 04
Programm • Scope:
106 Wohnungen • 106 apartments
Ort • Location: Frankfurt am Main
Geschossfläche (BGF) •
Floor area (gross): 11 000 m²
Bauherr • Client: Swiss Life AG
→ 249

Schwedler-Carré 01
Programm • Scope:
124 Wohnungen • 124 apartments
Ort • Location: Frankfurt am Main
Geschossfläche (BGF) •
Floor area (gross): 12 460 m²
Bauherr • Client: Max Baum Immobilien GmbH
→ 57

Langhaus
Programm • Scope:
40 Wohnungen • 40 apartments
Ort • Location: Freiburg
Geschossfläche (BGF) •
Floor area (gross): 5 230 m²
Bauherr • Client: Freiburger Stadtbau GmbH

Unicarré
Programm • Scope: 140 Wohnungen, Gewerbe, Kita • 140 apartments, commercial units, nursery school
Ort • Location: Freiburg
Geschossfläche (BGF) •
Floor area (gross): 17 260 m²
Bauherr • Client: Bauverein Breisgau e. G.

Rheinufer 02
Programm • Scope:
91 Wohnungen • 91 apartments
Ort • Location: Ludwigshafen am Rhein
Geschossfläche (BGF) •
Floor area (gross): 11 630 m²
Bauherr • Client: Weisenburger Projekt GmbH

2016

Windeckstraße
Programm • Scope:
48 Wohnungen • 48 apartments
Ort • Location: Frankfurt am Main
Geschossfläche (BGF) •
Floor area (gross): 6 500 m²
Bauherr • Client: Quartier East GmbH
→ 193

Adickesallee
Programm • Scope: 332 Wohnungen, Café • 332 apartments, café
Ort • Location: Frankfurt am Main
Geschossfläche (BGF) •
Floor area (gross): 14 500 m²
Bauherr • Client: RMW Wohnungsgesellschaft Frankfurt II GmbH
→ 177

Philosophicum
Programm • Scope: 238 Appartements, Kita, Café • 238 studio apartments, nursery school, café
Ort • Location: Frankfurt am Main
Geschossfläche (BGF) •
Floor area (gross): 12 130 m²
Bauherr • Client: RMW Wohnungsgesellschaft Frankfurt II GmbH
→ 275

Riedberg 03
Programm • Scope:
71 Wohnungen • 71 apartments
Ort • Location: Frankfurt am Main
Geschossfläche (BGF) •
Floor area (gross): 9 210 m²
Bauherr • Client: GWH Bauprojekte GmbH

Französische Allee
Programm • Scope:
57 Wohnungen • 57 apartments
Ort • Location: Hanau
Geschossfläche (BGF) •
Floor area (gross): 5 820 m²
Bauherr • Client: Baugesellschaft Hanau GmbH
→ 217

Schwarzwaldblock
Programm • Scope:
235 Wohnungen • 235 apartments
Ort • Location: Mannheim
Geschossfläche (BGF) •
Floor area (gross): 26 030 m²
Bauherr • Client: Baugenossenschaft Spar- und Bauverein 1895 Mannheim eG
→ 45

2015

Campus Bockenheim
Programm • Scope: 58 Wohnungen, Supermarkt • 58 apartments, supermarket
Ort • Location: Frankfurt am Main
Geschossfläche (BGF) •
Floor area (gross): 7 120 m²
Bauherr • Client: ABG Frankfurt Holding
→ 137

2014

Europaviertel E3
Programm • Scope:
75 Wohnungen • 75 apartments
Ort • Location: Frankfurt am Main
Geschossfläche (BGF) •
Floor area (gross): 10 610 m²
Bauherr • Client: Weisenburger Gewerbe + Wohnbau GmbH

Rheinufer 01
Programm • Scope:
72 Wohnungen • 72 apartments
Ort • Location: Ludwigshafen am Rhein
Geschossfläche (BGF) •
Floor area (gross): 9 130 m²
Bauherr • Client: Weisenburger Gewerbe + Wohnbau GmbH

2013

Sandweg
Programm • Scope: 31 Wohnungen, Doppelhaus, Ladeneinheit •
31 apartments, two semi-detached houses, shop unit
Ort • Location: Frankfurt am Main
Geschossfläche (BGF) •
Floor area (gross): 4 620 m²
Bauherr • Client: GeRo Sandweg-Projektentwicklungs GmbH & Co. KG
→ 161

Westgarten 02
Programm • Scope:
39 Wohnungen • 39 apartments
Ort • Location: Frankfurt am Main
Geschossfläche (BGF) •
Floor area (gross): 4 410 m²
Bauherr • Client: Max Baum Immobilien GmbH/General Deutschland Holding AG

Wohnen auf Naxos •
Living on Naxos
Programm • Scope:
116 Wohnungen • 116 apartments
Ort • Location: Frankfurt am Main
Geschossfläche (BGF) •
Floor area (gross): 15 000 m²
Bauherr • Client: ABG Frankfurt Holding
→ 169

Mainzeile
Programm • Scope:
178 Wohnungen • 178 apartments
Ort • Location: Offenbach am Main
Geschossfläche (BGF) •
Floor area (gross): 21 540 m²
Bauherr • Client: ABG Frankfurt Holding
→ 241

2012

Gemeindezentrum •
Community Centre
Programm • Scope: 14 Wohnungen, kirchliches Gemeindezentrum mit Büros • 14 apartments, church community centre with offices
Ort • Location: Frankfurt am Main
Geschossfläche (BGF) •
Floor area (gross): 1 740 m²
Bauherr • Client: Evangelischer Regionalverband Frankfurt am Main
→ 101

Riedberg 01
Programm • Scope:
149 Wohnungen • 149 apartments
Ort • Location: Frankfurt am Main
Geschossfläche (BGF) •
Floor area (gross): 16 030 m²
Bauherr • Client: Swiss Life AG

Welfenstraße
Programm • Scope:
157 Wohnungen • 157 apartments
Ort • Location: München
Geschossfläche (BGF) •
Floor area (gross): 16 850 m²
Bauherr • Client: Bayerische Bau und Immobilien GmbH & Co. KG

Brunostraße
Programm • Scope:
104 Wohnungen • 104 apartments
Ort • Location: Würzburg
Geschossfläche (BGF) •
Floor area (gross): 10 680 m²
Bauherr • Client: Stadtbau Würzburg GmbH

2011

Idsteiner Straße
Programm • Scope:
22 Wohnungen • 22 apartments
Ort • Location: Frankfurt am Main
Geschossfläche (BGF) •
Floor area (gross): 2 130 m²
Bauherr • Client: ABG Frankfurt Holding

Wohn- und Geschäftshaus R7 • R7 apartment and office block
Programm • Scope:
34 Wohnungen, Geschäftsräume •
34 apartments, offices
Ort • Location: Mannheim
Geschossfläche (BGF) •
Floor area (gross): 4 800 m²
Bauherr • Client: Baugenossenschaft Spar- und Bauverein 1895 Mannheim eG
→ 201

2010

Europaviertel Westparc
Programm • Scope:
59 Wohnungen • 59 apartments
Ort • Location: Frankfurt am Main
Geschossfläche (BGF) •
Floor area (gross): 6 560 m²
Bauherr • Client: GWH Gemeinnützige Wohnungsbaugesellschaft mbH Hessen

Hansaallee
Programm • Scope:
45 Wohnungen • 45 apartments
Ort • Location: Frankfurt am Main
Geschossfläche (BGF) •
Floor area (gross): 5 000 m²
Bauherr • Client: ABG Frankfurt Holding

Kepler-Residenz
Programm • Scope:
27 Wohnungen • 27 apartments
Ort • Location: Frankfurt am Main
Geschossfläche (BGF) •
Floor area (gross): 4 500 m²
Bauherr • Client: GeRo Real Estate

Lyoner Straße 01
Programm • Scope:
98 Wohnungen • 98 apartments
Ort • Location: Frankfurt am Main
Geschossfläche (BGF) •
Floor area (gross): 9 840 m²
Bauherr • Client: Dreyer Vierte Verwaltungsgesellschaft mbH
→ 263

Mörfelder Landstraße
Programm • Scope: 56 Wohnungen, Kita, Läden, Gewerbe • 56 apartments, nursery school, shops, commercial units
Ort • Location: Frankfurt am Main
Geschossfläche (BGF) •
Floor area (gross): 9 840 m²
Bauherr • Client: Max Baum Immobilien GmbH

Haus 08
Programm • Scope:
125 Wohnungen • 125 apartments
Ort • Location: Halle (Saale)
Geschossfläche (BGF) •
Floor area (gross): 7 300 m²
Bauherr • Client: GWG Halle-Neustadt
→ 315

2009

Campo am Bornheimer Depot
Programm • Scope: 150 Wohnungen, Gewerbe • 150 apartments, commercial units
Ort • Location: Frankfurt am Main
Geschossfläche (BGF) •
Floor area (gross): 5 740 m²
Bauherr • Client: ABG Frankfurt Holding

2008

Wohnen im Park •
Houses in the park
Programm • Scope:
32 Wohnungen • 32 apartments
Ort • Location: Frankfurt am Main
Geschossfläche (BGF) •
Floor area (gross): 4 830 m²
Bauherr • Client: Frank Heimbau
→ 229

Ostendstraße
Programm • Scope:
16 Wohnungen • 16 apartments
Ort • Location: Frankfurt am Main
Geschossfläche (BGF) •
Floor area (gross): 1 910 m²
Bauherr • Client: Mainterra GmbH
→ 185

2007

Haus 06
Programm • Scope:
36 Wohnungen • 36 apartments
Ort • Location: Leinefelde
Geschossfläche (BGF) •
Floor area (gross): 2 240 m²
Bauherr • Client: LWG Leinefelde
→ 291

2006

**Wohnanlage Voltastraße •
Voltastraße residential
development**
Programm • Scope:
160 Wohnungen • 160 apartments
Ort • Location: Frankfurt am Main
Geschossfläche (BGF) •
Floor area (gross): 14 920 m²
Bauherr • Client: ABG Frankfurt Holding
→ 73

Haus 05
Programm • Scope:
80 Wohnungen • 80 apartments
Ort • Location: Leinefelde
Geschossfläche (BGF) •
Floor area (gross): 2 640 m²
Bauherr • Client: LWG Leinefelde
→ 291

2005

Hardtberger Gärten
Programm • Scope:
68 Wohnungen • 68 apartments
Ort • Location: Königstein
Bauherr • Client: Vivacon

**Wohnsiedlung am
Floßhafen • Housing Estate
Floßhafen**
Ort • Location: Mainz
Bauherr • Client: Schollmayer
Vermögensverwaltung GmbH

Westgarten 01
Programm • Scope:
70 Wohnungen, Supermarkt, Ladenzeile • 70 apartments, supermarket, row of shops
Ort • Location: Frankfurt am Main
Geschossfläche (BGF) •
Floor area (gross): 9 250 m²
Bauherr • Client: Max Baum
Immobilien GmbH
→ 113

2004

Haus 07
Programm • Scope:
150 Wohnungen • 150 apartments
Geschossfläche (BGF) •
Floor area (gross): 4 200 m²
Ort • Location: Leinefelde
Bauherr • Client: WVL Wohnungs-Verwaltungs-GmbH Leinefelde
→ 307

2003

Haus 04
Programm • Scope:
20 Wohnungen • 20 apartments
Geschossfläche (BGF) •
Floor area (gross): 1 580 m²
Ort • Location: Leinefelde
Bauherr • Client: LWG Leinefelde
→ 291

2002

Haus 03
Programm • Scope:
32 Wohnungen • 32 apartments
Geschossfläche (BGF) •
Floor area (gross): 2 270 m²
Ort • Location: Leinefelde
Bauherr • Client: LWG Leinefelde
→ 291

Schulumbau • School
Ort • Location: Leinefelde
Bauherr • Client: Stadt Leinefelde

**Neugestaltung Vorplatz
Obereichsfeldhalle •
Restructuring forecourt
Obereichsfeldhalle**
Ort • Location: Leinefelde
Bauherr • Client: Stadt Leinefelde

Umbau Foyer Obereichsfeldhalle • Conversion foyer Obereichsfeldhalle
Ort • Location: Leinefelde
Bauherr • Client: Stadt Leinefelde

2001

Haus 02
Programm • Scope:
64 Wohnungen • apartments
Ort • Location: Leinefelde
Geschossfläche (BGF) •
Floor area (gross): 4 380 m²
Bauherr • Client: LWG Leinefelde
→ 291

**Gemeindehalle •
Community hall**
Ort • Location: Breitenholz
Bauherr • Client: Stadt Breitenholz

Plattenbautransformation
Programm • Scope:
137 Wohnungen • 137 apartments
Ort • Location: Wismar
Bauherr • Client: Wobau

2000

Wohnstift • Residential home
Ort • Location: Wetzlar
Bauherr • Client: Residia

1999

**Bürogebäude Rentaco •
Office building Rentaco**
Ort • Location: Berlin
Bauherr • Client: Rentaco AG

Haus 01
Programm • Scope:
120 Wohnungen • 120 apartments
Ort • Location: Leinefelde
Bauherr • Client: LWG Leinefelde
→ 291

1997

**Sanierung und Umbau
Bilderbogenpassage •
Renovation and conversion
Bilderbogenpassage**
Ort • Location: Neu-Ruppin
Bauherr • Client: Rentaco AG

**Fassadenplanung Lindenzentrum • Facade planning
Lindenzentrum**
Programm • Scope:
Einkaufszentrum • Shopping centre
Ort • Location: Neuruppin
Bauherr • Client: Rentaco AG

Lindenarkade
Programm • Scope: Wohnungen,
Büros (Sanierung, Um- und Neubau) •
Apartments, offices (renovation,
conversion, new construction)
Ort • Location: Potsdam
Bauherr • Client: Rentaco AG

Solitär 02
Programm • Scope:
42 Wohnungen • 42 apartments
Geschossfläche (BGF) •
Floor area (gross): 2 800 m²
Ort • Location: Frankfurt am Main
Bauherr • Client: HPI Heberger

1995

**Wohnstift für betreutes
Wohnen • Residential
home for assisted living**
Ort • Location: Salzgitter
Bauherr • Client: Rentaco AG

1993

**Umbau Wohn- und
Geschäftshaus • Conversion
apartment and office block**
Ort • Location: Darmstadt
Bauherr • Client: privat • private

**Büro- und Produktionsgebäude Conitec • Conitec
office and production building**
Geschossfläche (BGF) •
Floor area (gross): 500 m²
Ort • Location: Dieburg (Odenwald)
Bauherr • Client: Conitec Datensysteme

**Umbau Gründerzentrum •
Start-up centre conversion**
Ort • Location: Stendal
Bauherr • Client: Stadt Stendal

1992

**Umbau Bankgebäude •
Conversion bank building**
Ort • Location: Görlitz
Bauherr • Client: Dresdner Bank

**Hotel (Sanierung und Umbau
eines Altbaus) • Hotel
(renovation and conversion
of an old building)**
Geschossfläche (BGF) •
Floor area (gross): 600 m²
Ort • Location: Görlitz
Bauherr • Client: privat

**Umbau Bankgebäude •
Bank building conversion**
Ort • Location: Halle (Saale)
Bauherr • Client: Dresdner Bank

**Umbau Bankgebäude •
Bank building conversion**
Ort • Location: Meißen
Bauherr • Client: Dresdner Bank

**Neubau Bankgebäude •
New construction bank building**
Ort • Location: Pirna
Bauherr • Client: Dresdner Bank

1991

**Wohn- und Geschäftshaus •
Apartment and office building**
Geschossfläche (BGF) •
Floor area (gross): 900 m²
Ort • Location: Kaiserslautern
Bauherr • Client: privat

1990

**Umbau und Erweiterung
eines Hotels • Conversion
and extension of a hotel**
Geschossfläche (BGF) •
Floor area (gross): 500 m²
Ort • Location: Darmstadt
Bauherr • Client: privat • private

**Erweiterung Wohn- und
Geschäftshaus • Extension
apartment and office building**
Geschossfläche (BGF) •
Floor area (gross): 500 m²
Ort • Location: Höchst im Odenwald
Bauherr • Client: privat • private

1988

**Umbau und Erweiterung
Einfamilienhaus •
Single-family house
conversion and extension**
Geschossfläche (BGF) •
Floor area (gross): 100 m²
Ort • Location: Imsbach (Pfalz)
Bauherr • Client: privat • private

1987

**Umbau Einfamilienhaus •
Single-family house
conversion**
Geschossfläche (BGF) •
Floor area (gross): 150 m²
Ort • Location: Heidelberg
Bauherr • Client: privat • private

**Haus Müller
(Erweiterung • Extension)**
Geschossfläche (BGF) •
Floor area (gross): 100 m²
Ort • Location: Lohnsfeld (Pfalz)
Bauherr • Client: privat • private

1986

**Villenumbau •
Villa conversion**
Geschossfläche (BGF) •
Floor area (gross): 220 m²
Ort • Location: Siena, Italien
Bauherr • Client: Carla and
Stefano Freato

2019
— DAM Preis für Architektur 2020, Shortlist, Wohnhaus Schloßstraße, Frankfurt am Main

2018
— German Design Award, Nominierung, Oskar Residence
— Martin-Elsaesser-Plakette des Bundes Deutscher Architekten im Lande Hessen für Philosophicum, Frankfurt am Main

2017
— DAM Preis für Architektur 2018, Shortlist, Philosophicum, Frankfurt am Main
— Wüstenrot-Preis 2017, Nominierung, Philosophicum, Frankfurt am Main
— Fritz-Höger-Preis 2017, Nominierung, Philosophicum, Frankfurt am Main
— Iconic Award 2017 für Oskar Residence, Frankfurt am Main

2016
— Deutscher Bauherrenpreis für Wohnanlage Brunostraße, Würzburg

2015
— Staatspreis Baukultur Baden-Württemberg für Schwarzwaldblock, Mannheim (Nominierung)
— Deutscher Ziegelpreis, Sonderpreis für das Gemeindezentrum in Frankfurt am Main

2014
— Architekturpreis Auszeichnung vorbildlicher Bauten im Land Hessen für das Gemeindezentrum, Frankfurt am Main
— Architekturpreis »Beispielhaftes Bauen 2007–2013« der Architektenkammer Baden-Württemberg für das Wohn- und Geschäftshaus R7, Mannheim

2013
— Umweltpreis der Stadt Mannheim für das Wohn- und Geschäftshaus R7
— Architekturpreis Sachsen, engere Wahl, Haus 08, Halle (Saale)

2012
— Hannes-Meyer-Preis, engere Wahl, Haus 08, Halle (Saale)
— Deutscher Bauherrenpreis, besondere Anerkennung für Schwarzwaldblock, Mannheim
— AIT Award 2012, 2. Preis für Wohnhochhaus Lyoner Straße, Frankfurt am Main

2011
— Hugo-Häring-Auszeichnung für Schwarzwaldblock, Mannheim
— The Philippe Rotthier European Prize for Architecture für Haus 08, Halle (Saale)
— Green Building Award für Passivhaus Campo am Bornheimer Depot, Frankfurt am Main
— Deutscher Bauherrenpreis, besondere Anerkennung für Haus 08, Halle (Saale), Schwarzwaldblock, Mannheim und Lyoner Straße 01, Frankfurt am Main

2010
— Deutscher Städtebaupreis für Campo am Bornheimer Depot, Frankfurt am Main (Belobigung)
— Heinze Architekten Award für Wohnhochhaus Lyoner Straße 01, Frankfurt am Main

2009
— Architekturpreis Ziegel Zentrum Süd für Westgarten 01, Frankfurt am Main
— Nationaler Preis für integrierte Stadtentwicklung und Baukultur für Campo am Bornheimer Depot, Frankfurt am Main

2008
— Fritz-Höger-Preis für Backsteinarchitektur für Wohnanlage Voltastraße und Westgarten 01, Frankfurt am Main (Nominierung)
— best architects 08 für Haus 05, Leinefelde
— ECOLA Award, Sonderpreis für CO2-optimiertes Bauen

2007
— World Habitat Award (mit Zukunftswerkstatt Leinefelde)
— best architects 07 für Wohnanlage Voltastraße, Frankfurt am Main
— Architekturpreis »Zukunft Wohnen 2007«, Haus 05, Leinefelde
— Deutscher Fassadenpreis für Haus 05, Leinefelde (Anerkennung)
— Deutscher Bauherrenpreis »Modernisierung« (Besondere Anerkennung)

2006
— Preis der Baukultur Thüringen für Haus 01–07, Leinefelde
— Gestaltungspreis der Wüstenrot-Stiftung »Umbau im Bestand« für Haus 07, Leinefelde

2005
— Architekturpreis der Architektenkammer Thüringen für Haus 04, Leinefelde
— Innovationspreis der Thüringer Wohnungswirtschaft für Haus 07, Leinefelde
— Sir-Robert-Matthew-Preis der International Union of Architects (UIA) für Stadtumbau Ost, Leinefelde
— Deutscher Bauherrenpreis für Haus 07, Leinefelde
— Deutscher Architekturpreis für Haus 07, Leinefelde (engere Wahl)

2004
— Europäischer Städtebaupreis für Stadtumbau Ost, Leinefelde

2003
— Deutscher Städtebaupreis für Stadtumbau Ost, Leinefelde
— Deutscher Bauherrenpreis für Haus 03, Leinefelde

2001
— Deutscher Bauherrenpreis für Haus 01, Leinefelde

2000
— Staatspreis für Architektur und Städtebau Thüringen, Anerkennung

---

2019
— "DAM Preis für Architektur 2020", shortlist, Schloßstraße apartment block, Frankfurt am Main

2018
— German Design Award, nomination, for Oskar Residence
— "Martin-Elsaesser-Plakette" of the Bund Deutscher Architekten in Hessen for the Philosophicum, Frankfurt am Main

2017
— "DAM Preis for Architektur 2018", shortlist, Philosophicum, Frankfurt am Main;
— "Wüstenrot-Preis 2017", nomination, Philosophicum, Frankfurt am Main
— "Fritz-Höger-Preis 2017", nomination, Philosophicum, Frankfurt am Main
— Iconic Award 2017 for Oskar Residence, Frankfurt am Main

2016
— "Deutscher Bauherrenpreis" for the Brunostraße residential complex, Würzburg

2015
— "Staatspreis Baukultur Baden-Württemberg" for Schwarzwaldblock, Mannheim (nomination)
— "Deutscher Ziegelpreis", Special Award for the community centre, Frankfurt am Main

2014
— "Architekturpreis Auszeichnung vorbildlicher Bauten im Land Hessen" for the community centre, Frankfurt am Main
— Architectural award "Beispielhaftes Bauen 2007–2013" of the Chamber of Architects of Baden-Württemberg for the R7 apartment and office block, Mannheim

2013
— "Umweltpreis der Stadt Mannheim" for the R7 apartment and office block, Mannheim
— "Architekturpreis Sachsen", shortlisted, for House 08, Halle (Saale)

2012
— "Hannes-Meyer-Preis", shortlisted, for House 08, Halle (Saale)
— "Deutscher Bauherrenpreis", Special Mention for Schwarzwaldblock, Mannheim
— AIT Award 2012, 2nd Prize for the Lyoner Straße residential high-rise, Frankfurt am Main

2011
— "Hugo-Häring-Auszeichnung" for Schwarzwaldblock, Mannheim
— Philippe Rotthier European Prize for Architecture for House 08, Halle (Saale)
— Green Building Award for the Campo passive building at Bornheimer Depot, Frankfurt am Main
— "Deutscher Bauherrenpreis", Special Mention for House 08, Halle (Saale), Schwarzwaldblock, Mannheim, and Lyoner Straße 01, Frankfurt am Main

2010
— "Deutscher Städtebaupreis" for Campo at Bornheimer Depot, Frankfurt am Main (Commendation)
— Heinze Architekten Award for the Lyoner Straße 01 residential high-rise, Frankfurt am Main

2009
— "Architekturpreis Ziegel Zentrum Süd" for Westgarten 01, Frankfurt am Main;
— "Nationaler Preis for integrierte Stadtentwicklung und Baukultur" for Campo at Bornheimer Depot, Frankfurt am Main

2008
— "Fritz-Höger-Preis for Backsteinarchitektur" for the Voltastraße residential development and Westgarten 01, Frankfurt am Main (nomination)
— best architects 08 for House 05, Leinefelde
— ECOLA Award, Special Award for carbon-optimised building

2007
— World Habitat Award (with Future Workshop Leinefelde);
— best architects 07 for the Voltastraße residential development, Frankfurt am Main;
— Architectural award "Zukunft Wohnen 2007", House 05, Leinefelde
— "Deutscher Fassadenpreis" for House 05, Leinefelde (Special Mention)
— "Deutscher Bauherrenpreis" for modernisation (Special Mention)

2006
— "Preis der Baukultur Thüringen" for House 01–07, Leinefelde
— "Gestaltungspreis der Wüstenrot-Stiftung" for renovation for House 07, Leinefelde

2005
— "Architekturpreis der Architektenkammer Thüringen" for House 04, Leinefelde
— "Innovationspreis der Thüringer Wohnungswirtschaft" for House 07, Leinefelde
— Sir Robert Matthew Award of the International Union of Architects (UIA) for "Stadtumbau Ost", Leinefelde
— "Deutscher Bauherrenpreis" for House 07, Leinefelde
— "Deutscher Architekturpreis" for House 07, Leinefelde (shortlisted)

2004
— European Urban & Regional Planning Award for "Stadtumbau Ost", Leinefelde

2003
— "Deutscher Städtebaupreis" for "Stadtumbau Ost", Leinefelde
— "Deutscher Bauherrenpreis" for House 03, Leinefelde

2001
— "Deutscher Bauherrenpreis" for House 01, Leinefelde

2000
— "Staatspreis for Architektur und Städtebau Thüringen", Special Mention

Alle Pläne, Grundrisse und Schnitte • All plans and sections © Stefan Forster Architekten. Aufbereitung von • by Dorna Khan Mohammadi und • and Christina Wüst.

Umschlag • Cover: Lisa Farkas
1–16: Lisa Farkas
46, oben links • top left: Stefan Forster
46, unten links • bottom left: Lisa Farkas
46/47, Mitte • centre: Rhein-Neckar-Zeitung/Foto • photo: Alfred Gerold
47, rechts • right, 1–3: © Google Earth, 2020 AeroWest
49–56: Lisa Farkas
58, links • left, 1–8: Lisa Farkas
58–59: Mitte, oben und unten • centre, top and bottom: Stefan Forster
59, rechts • right: Max Baum Immobilien/Visualisierung • visualisation: Architektur Darstellung michael behrendt/ Geobasisdaten • geobase data: © Stadtvermessungsamt Frankfurt am Main, Stand 07.2014
61–72: Lisa Farkas
74–75: Stefan Forster
77–81: Jean-Luc Valentin
82–83: Lisa Farkas
84: Jean-Luc Valentin
86–87: Yvonne Schucht
89–92: Lisa Farkas
102: Stefan Forster
105–112: Lisa Farkas
114, Links, oben und unten • left, top and bottom: Jean-Luc Valentin
114–115, Mitte • centre: Stefan Forster
115, rechts, 1–3: Jean-Luc Valentin
117: Jean-Luc Valentin
118–119: Lisa Farkas
120–121: Jean-Luc Valentin
122: Lisa Farkas
123–124: Jean-Luc Valentin
126, links • left: Lisa Farkas
126–127, Mitte, oben und unten • centre, top and bottom: Lisa Farkas
127, rechts, oben und unten • right, top and bottom: Yvonne Schucht
129–136: Lisa Farkas
138–139: Gerald Diezel
141–148: Lisa Farkas
150–151, links • left: Institut für Stadtgeschichte Frankfurt am Main (ISG FFM), S8-Stpl Nr. 1873, Ravenstein
150–151, Mitte, oben und unten • centre, top and bottom: Stefan Forster Architekten
151, rechts • right: Lisa Farkas
153–160: Lisa Farkas
163: Yvonne Schucht
165–168: Lisa Farkas
170, oben links • top left: Institut für Stadtgeschichte Frankfurt am Main (ISG FFM), ISG FFM S7A Nr. 1998-30223, NN
170, unten links • bottom left: Institut für Stadtgeschichte Frankfurt am Main (ISG FFM), ISG FFM S7A Nr. 1998-30224, NN
170–171, Mitte oben • centre top: Institut für Stadtgeschichte Frankfurt am Main (ISG FFM)
170–171, Mitte, mittig und unten • centre, centre and bottom: Stefan Forster
171, rechts, oben und unten • right, top and bottom: Lisa Farkas
173–176: Lisa Farkas
179: Frankfurter Allgemeine Zeitung, Rainer Schulze, 20.5.2014 © Alle Rechte vorbehalten. Frankfurter Allgemeine Zeitung GmbH, Frankfurt. Zur Verfügung gestellt vom Frankfurter Allgemeine Archiv.
181–184: Lisa Farkas
186–187: Lisa Farkas
189–192: Jean-Luc Valentin

194, links, oben und unten • left, top and bottom: Yvonne Schucht
194–195, Mitte, oben und unten • centre, top and bottom: Stefan Forster
195, rechts, oben und unten • right, top and bottom: Benjamin Semmler/Frankfurt Babylon
197–200: Lisa Farkas
202, oben links • top left: Stefan Forster
202–203, Mitte und rechts • centre and right: Lisa Farkas
205–208: Lisa Farkas
210, links oben • top left: Stefan Forster Architekten
210–211, Mitte links, oben und unten • centre left, top and bottom: Stadt Düsseldorf, Vermessungs- und Katasteramt, Lizenz-Nr.: 024 2020
210–211, Mitte rechts, oben und unten • centre right, top and bottom: Stefan Forster Architekten
211, rechts, 1–3 • right 1–3: Lisa Farkas
213–215: Lisa Farkas
218, links oben • top left: Repro-Center, Stadt Hanau
218–219, Mitte links, oben und unten • centre left, top and bottom: Stadtplanungsamt Hanau
218–219, Mitte rechts, 1–3 • centre right, 1–3: Yvonne Schucht
219, rechts • right: Lisa Farkas
221: Lisa Farkas
222–223: Baugesellschaft Hanau/ Günter Gottlieb
224: Lisa Farkas
230, links • left: Frankfurter Allgemeine Zeitung, 5.7.2006 © Alle Rechte vorbehalten. Frankfurter Allgemeine Zeitung GmbH, Frankfurt. Zur Verfügung gestellt vom Frankfurter Allgemeine Archiv.
230–231, Mitte und rechts • centre and right: Lisa Farkas
233: Lisa Farkas
234–231: Jean-Luc Valentin
236: Lisa Farkas
237: Jean-Luc Valentin
238–236: Lisa Farkas
242, links und Mitte • left and centre: Lisa Farkas
243: Stefan Forster
245–248: Lisa Farkas
250–251, Geobasisdaten • geobase data: © Stadtvermessungsamt Frankfurt am Main, Stand 06.2017
253–256: Lisa Farkas
264, links, 1–3 • left, 1–3: Stefan Forster Architekten
264–265, Mitte • centre: Stefan Forster Architekten
267–270: Jean-Luc Valentin
271: Lisa Farkas
272–274: Jean-Luc Valentin
276, links, oben und unten • left, top and bottom: Lutz Kleinhans • Kramer Archiv
276–277, Mitte links • centre left: Frankfurter Allgemeine Zeitung, Rainer Schulze, 4.12.2014 © Alle Rechte vorbehalten. Frankfurter Allgemeine Zeitung GmbH, Frankfurt. Zur Verfügung gestellt vom Frankfurter Allgemeine Archiv.
276–277, Mitte rechts und rechts • centre right and right: Lisa Farkas
279–290: Lisa Farkas
292–293: Jean-Luc Valentin
295–305: Jean-Luc Valentin
308–309: Mark magazine/Fotos • photos: Jean-Luc Valentin
311–314: Jean-Luc Valentin
316, oben links • top left: Stefan Forster Architekten
316–317, Mitte • centre: Stefan Forster Architekten
317: Jean-Luc Valentin
319–322: Jean-Luc Valentin

Herausgeber • Editor:
Stefan Forster

Konzept • Concept:
Sandra Doeller, Benjamin Pfeifer

Projektleitung und Texte •
Project lead and texts:
Benjamin Pfeifer

Bildredaktion • Image editing:
Lisa Farkas, Benjamin Pfeifer

Lektorat und Korrektorat •
Copy editing and proofreading:
Enrico Wagner, www.pertext.de

Übersetzung und Endkorrektur •
Translation and proofreading:
Ingrid Taylor

Gestaltung • Design:
Bureau Sandra Doeller,
Sandra Doeller, Merle Petsch

Lithografie • Lithography:
Peter Schladoth

Druck und Bindung •
Printing and binding:
Offsetdruckerei Karl Grammlich

© 2020 Stefan Forster Architekten,
Frankfurt am Main, und • and
Park Books AG, Zürich

© für die Texte: die Autorinnen und
Autoren • for the texts: the authors

© für die Bilder: die Künstlerinnen und
Künstler • for the images: the artists

Mit freundlicher Unterstützung
der Klinkermanufakturen Janinhoff
und Gillrath.

With the kind support of the brick
manufacturers Janinhoff and Gillrath.

Park Books
Niederdorfstrasse 54
8001 Zürich
Schweiz • Switzerland
www.park-books.com

Park Books wird vom Bundesamt für
Kultur mit einem Strukturbeitrag für die
Jahre 2016–2020 unterstützt.
Park Books is being supported by the
Federal Office of Culture with a general
subsidy for the years 2016–2020.

Alle Rechte vorbehalten; kein Teil
dieses Werks darf in irgendeiner Form
ohne vorherige schriftliche Genehmigung des Verlags reproduziert oder
unter Verwendung elektronischer
Systeme verarbeitet, vervielfältigt oder
verbreitet werden.
All rights reserved; no part of this
publication may be reproduced, stored
in a retrieval system or transmitted
in any form or by any means, electronic,
mechanical, photocopying, recording,
or otherwise, without the prior written
consent of the publisher.

ISBN 978-3-03860-180-7